NO MORE SECRETS

NO MORE SECRETS

FROM HURT NEVER TOLD TO TRANSFORMATIONAL TRUTH

a memoir

ADAM VOLANT

ACV PUBLISHING

Published by Adam C. Volant
Copyright © 2024 by ACV Publishing

Library of Congress Cataloging-in-Publication Data
ISBN: 979-8-9904689-0-0
LCCN: 2024906775

First Printing September 2024
Printed in the United States of America

Cover Design: Jeff Miller, Faceout Studio
Interior Design: Zoe Norvell
Editor: Elaine Barnes

This book is dedicated to those whose hurts remain, sealed by our footsteps seeking peace in our broken existence.

To those who shed the uniform but remain tied to the torment of war and internal battle of PTSD.

For the heroes of my life who are not fallen but whose names and service should never be forgotten.

SGT Tracy Hampton, USA

1LT Terry Plunk, USA

LT Ray Dyer, USN

CPT Mark McCarthy, USAF

LT Mark Wilson, USN

CPT Mark Lamb, USA

LTC John Monihan, ARNG

My family, for their patience in this journey and exploration of transformation. Especially to my wife whose encouragement and valued critique shone light on more important truths.

Elaine, longtime friend and sister in this effort. Your words, capable hands, and passionate effort made all the difference.

McKinley Burke, your unselfish and strong arm reached out to me when the alarm sounded in a moment of pain. You revealed your heart, sealed our brotherhood, and saved my life in ways that I have never shared. Until I find you on the terrestrial level or meet you in heaven, I pray God gives you peace in measure with the love you quietly shared with those fortunate to serve alongside you.

Wade, your partnership and prayer in the storm guided a young man to see God more clearly. I thank you for the verses of "Walk On" and smile when I think of singing together in the back of a truck.

TABLE OF CONTENTS

Introduction

I REMEMBER THE FIRST TIME I heard someone say that God was omniscient, that He knew all things, that there was nothing outside of His knowledge or control. I was confounded by this statement, not by the enormity of what it suggested, but rather by the injustice it proved.

At six years old I was touched by a family friend, a recurring molestation that continued until I was thirteen. There was no one to tell, and so I did what I was told to do. I kept the secret of this indignity and the pain it caused. I kept that secret until decades later.

Lost for direction after high school, I joined the military seeking purpose and a way to break out of the pervasive pattern of mediocrity that defined my life. Headed for nowhere, I joined the Army to get somewhere, even though I did not know where that was or who I truly was in making that decision. But a new start, a uniform, and maybe some successes might cover the hole I felt inside. Or so I thought.

Along the way I often stumbled on the irreconcilable scar from a six-year-old whose pajamas did not fit. Why had I never told anyone? Why did I not do more to stop being abused? Why did I allow him to take off my clothes and innocence? Why did this happen to me? What was wrong with me? And what is wrong with the world if a God can allow this to happen? Even worse, if the all-knowing God knew it was going to happen before it happened, how could He allow something so terrible to be weighed against one boy? If it was punishment, what had I done to deserve this lifelong mark and infection?

I kept the secret. I was faithful to the truth when it served to tear me down and make me stutter in speech, cringe with crowds, and fear being exposed. I kept the secret that it hurt me in ways I have yet to describe or understand. I kept the secret that I found ways to dull the memory with alcohol and drugs. I also kept the secret that I was lost without a way to connect my experience with the loving God that I heard about: the One that knew all things and yet allowed me to be spoiled in this way. Secretly, I resented Him and looked for other ways to hide.

The military proved to be a place where I could try, fail, and succeed. It was a great cover for what was inside. There was adversity, but there were achievements too, stories and a life that seemed to overshadow the experience of a young boy. I sought the challenges that would earn me a true badge of courage, something that would serve as a sign that I was not dented, that I was undisturbed and truly capable.

The military gave me new titles and recognition. New places and new people. Eventually I was chosen for work that was highly specialized and dealt with some of the most valuable secrets of our national security. There was a grueling process to be credentialed and have access to highly classified information. I had proven that I would keep that sacred oath to keep those secrets. I had joined the military at seventeen at the lowest entry rank, and by age fifty-six was promoted to general officer. The kid who left high school with a shrug jumped out of planes and helicopters, evolved through eleven promotions, had more than nine years in command of soldiers, and worked alongside offensive cyber operations that were approved at the presidential level. And the pathway for that ascension was teaming with professionals, learning from mistakes, and focusing intently on the job at hand.

Because I worked in the niche of cyber security, the clearance required a polygraph, a system of biometrics that are measured to detect my ability to protect secrets. And I knew too well that my whole life had prepared me to do just that: keep secrets. Boys do that. Teenagers keep secrets because they fear the exposure of their own flaws and deepest fears. And men keep secrets too; they cover and conceal the things they like least hoping the shadow and scars will not be seen. And general officers certainly keep secrets; it is the essence of their strategic work and the fuel for their continued service. When it is painful, or when the results of PTSD make it more complex, we seem to abide by the intolerance of a culture that abhors weakness. In the aggregate, we internalize and quietly suffer with corrosive effects over time.

Standing at a window in Maryland, I stared into an empty parking lot dazzled with colors from store lights. Awakened by a recurring nightmare of hopelessness, I contemplated my suicide and death with a burning desire to escape the shame of this world. I feared that soon the thin veil of military protocol, rank, and status would evaporate too suddenly and bare my own scars. I yearned for a way to describe what I felt and thought of songs whose lyrics might match my mood. I never found that melody, but what I had found was the central truth of my life and the only way I could face tomorrow. Barricaded into my own facade and belief system, I made the commitment to myself in the true hope that it might break someone else free. From that moment, I would live a life with no more secrets.

In the pages that follow, I'll share some of the scenes that shaped me most and remained under cover for many years. Although not in chronological order, the chapters are intended to bring different aspects to light. My story begins when I first discovered the light inside my darkness, how my abuse became the foundation for my own destruction. I've taken time to carefully reflect on details of how this happened to me and offer it as a humble profile that might alert others. My hope is to engage the reader in this story and perhaps compel them to consider their own shadows and experience. We all have secrets and experiences we do not want to reveal.

Clearly this is not a "how-to" and is not linear in the way the book describes why hurtful things happen, and especially why those circumstances are not punishment. To confide in others with our secrets, or to be willing to confess them, requires a very high level of trust and a confidence that grows organically. Part of the purpose of this book is to unveil a larger truth in many of us, and in doing so, give hope to each of us that labor and suffer alone.

Ugly as it is, being touched is not truly uncommon. Statistics report that one in four girls and one in six boys are somehow molested before the age of eighteen. If we believed that one of every six houses would burn in a fire, we would agree to have more firetrucks and first responders. This daunting stat, that our children continue to be disfigured by predators, is cast in numbers that likely understate the prevalence of sexual abuse because data is self-reported. And even uglier, we live in a world that is more likely to absorb this abuse amidst the noise and pace of our daily existence. What is perhaps most difficult to accept is that most of these cases of abuse occur with adults known to both the children and the parents. The trust shared within friends and within the loving circle of many homes has been invaded by an insider. That fact, absent the litany of cascading problems related to molestation, should cause us all to scrutinize where and who we trust. It cannot be a secret that there are threats we fail to see inside our families, friends, and people we know.

By speaking of the darkness in my life, I pledge to be truthful to the reader and their own experiences. While it would be grandiose to believe that these pages might be therapy, I have fervent hope that my confession will resonate enough to be a catalyst for good with others. Absent that, as an author I hold on to an equally valuable theme. My life with no more secrets is the only one that I can live and the one I believe I have been called to share with others.

I Am Sorry

AFTER SO MANY YEARS OF saying nothing, these chapters and my words should begin with an apology. We all have regrets in life and, while I have my portion, what I am sharing here I do not regret. Instead, I am sorry if the words strike in a way that they are not intended.

For those who actually know me in real life, I am sorry that these revelations will cast doubt on the impression you had of me. I am sorry that at some level my esteem has been diminished in your eyes with the knowledge that I am dented and made imperfect by these events. I add that I am also sorry if you feel somehow misled by me in what you thought you knew about me, and feel that I have somehow manipulated you. I should have had the courage to say all of this before now, and for that, I take refuge that I survived the journey and am sorry it was not said years ago.

I owe a special apology to my family. I am sorry if what is written spills into your lap or experience that we share. I have taken some time to ensure that details were not provided to indict or cast shadows on anyone. But I am sorry if you are offended or if you somehow believe that some things do not merit discussion or disclosure to others.

For those with whom I have served, I have taken careful steps to ensure that these words comply with both the letter and the spirit of security requirements for the government. I took special interest in submitting the entire text of these pages to the National Security Agency. I can certify that they take no issue with the information I will share. Having said that, I am sorry for those who hold a higher standard that requires that no information is shared. And I am sorry if you are bothered that some will conflate rightful requirements to secure information with my own personal issues with secrets in my life.

For those who share some overlap with the topics that I share, I am sorry that my thoughts in these areas likely do not match yours. I admit that I offer extremes and lean into my own experience with a bias that blinds me to what others experience or believe. I am sorry it does not match, not so much for the sake of equity as for the sake of providing you support and fellowship. So, to those who have been splattered, accept me saying I am sorry and please advantage any remnant of my thoughts to heal or help you.

Especially for Christian readers, I admit I have trouble even spelling "theologian" and am sorry my biblical references lack rigor. I have taken the time over some years to study the Bible with respect to the topics of this book, and I have consistently fallen short. As a reader and especially as a Christian, you deserve a more robust set of scripture references. I am sorry that the alignment I sought is incomplete and can only hope these pages spark a thirst for more correct application of the Bible.

Oddly, the list of sorry(s) is not complete, but perhaps the reader will appreciate my humble regret in sharing these words and my own experience. Having been to the pit of my own darkness and survived, I take some solace in praying that there will be enough truth or merit in what I offer to outweigh that which will be misunderstood, incorrect, or hurtful. I felt no need to publish a diary, but instead, felt compelled to share one fundamental truth that punctuates my own journey. I do pray it is helpful to others. And, if not, I pray the reader will know that I am sorry for not having met that modest and necessary standard.

Lastly, a special note and apology to the unwitting reader who came to these words through no direct intention or foreknowledge of the topic. I am sorry if reading this causes you in some way to have an irreconcilable concern for your children or for the malaise that has overcome our country with respect to these topics. We can believe for some time that the daily weather that brings only mist will never really get us wet. And yet we know the larger truth, that the moisture accumulates in such a way that we are actually soaked. That would be an assessment, perhaps an overly cautious one, of the environment we are in today. We have a daily mist, a pervasive and consistently small and almost invisible onslaught. We are many things, but likely no longer dry.

So here we stand, at the precipice of this book, or at the curb of our very street, knowing full well that we are immersed in a complex and saturated state. I am sorry that reading these words may disturb you. Please know that I write only with the hope that I am truthful to myself, obedient to what I know God has called me to, and with the modest expectation that these pages are a source of good or solace for others.

CHAPTER 1

Lights at Anne Arundel

I STOOD LOOKING OUT THE window into the colored lights that adorned Cinemark, the movie theater nested within Anne Arundel Mills Mall and shopping center in Maryland. Condensation showed on the window as my labored breathing mixed with tears. My heart raced and the ringing tinnitus, a blanket covering my hearing, screamed at a high pitch. Startled from sleep and now in full panic, I stared across the interstate into the complex array of bright lights. Reds and yellows shone with brilliance formed by moisture, intensity, and the flat canvas of empty parking spaces. Attempting to take a bigger recovery breath and exhale, I only shuttered to break down in the sobbing I had avoided for too long.

The colored lights of Anne Arundel formed brushstrokes created by rain that allowed the parking lot to reflect in red and orange lines. The scene was from a watercolor where one primary color is diluted as it spreads to another zone. Loud red streaks went from the ornate theater into the black and vacant palette of the parking lot. In my gaze into the window, I saw bright strokes of color that outlined shapes and moved when tears welled in my eyes. It was a kaleidoscope of sorts, the geometric shapes and view changing each time my eyes blinked to create another prism. I felt a fellowship with an earlier memory of my youth where I looked out the window through larger Christmas lights. The sadness of that day and abuse matched the early morning awakening I now had in Maryland.

How long had I feared the pursuit of the wolf, drawing me into a sullen surrender to my own brokenness? Pain, a catalyst for purpose, wore me to fray and in this moment, and in a recurring theme of many months, I longed for this to end. And for me to end with it. The hurt was too big and the pieces too fragmented to fit together. I longed for the quiet resolve to see the beast no more, and to rid myself from the shame and hopelessness.

The night was not special; it was more than five months into my sobriety and the journey to stop my slide and addiction. I had controlled the urges and filled my days with tasks to replace any torment or discontent. Nights were longer, but I had grown used to waking startled and unable to return to sleep. But this night was different. It was not just waking up; I was face to face with my greatest fear in fantastic color. It was a turning point where I thought most about bringing it all to an end.

The breath in my face had startled me awake in an urgent and violent reaction that drew me from bed, nearly falling to move from sleep to standing. The breath was forceful and came from a black wolf, a recurring dream that haunted me for years. The wolf moved over the dark cloudy sky and moved quickly to my face and neck. He had a low groan and with his exhale, the strong smell of bourbon poured over my face. The panic was immediate and the stench of liquor so strong that I never paused to consider if it was genuine. The reflex was instinctive, "get away, run from evil." In my panic it seemed the wolf had cornered me, and oddly, I feared the death that he seemed aimed to suggest. He was suspended in dark clouds and his eyes, the deepest and darkest part of his angry face, pierced into me.

The wolf had not always suggested my end. Tom began his spiraling lies by instilling a fear, and once that faulty premise took root, he laid the balance on me and my failure for being led to terrible things.

"What will anyone think if they know this about you?" It was sufficient to plant a seed of doubt that haunted me over many years. Could people see that I hesitated and was paralyzed by fear, that I suffered from stuttering until I was ten? Did they see the fracture of my personality and the absence of real meaning in my life? Did they know I was merely wandering from one moment to the next, always wondering how visible the damage done to me by this breach of my innocence was? The accumulation of those feelings that led to despair.

The secret I struggled to keep was not that I had been sexually molested by a man but, through his manipulation and suggestion, that I had a secret to hide. The fact that I had been spoiled while so young must be a secret, or so he suggested. If revealed, I knew it would unravel all the hurt that had been wound and unwound for so long. Shame covered me like a curtain. I lost an ability to resist from naivete and knew my lack of escape meant I was complicit. I wanted nothing but the touching to stop with all my soul. But I also feared the consequences. In all the years that followed, I often wondered if my actions were covering for me and that my secret was safe. Absent anything else, I had to keep the secret.

The best way to silence the ruminations of my mind was to end the pattern and me. The dark place that lingered that appeared over many years had become dominant in my thoughts. As I thought about death, I first considered how my family would not be burdened when my cover came apart. The intricate seams of my life, sewn together by more lies and silence, may one day come apart and make me truly bare. I envisioned the humiliation that I felt imagining that my frailty would be seen, and I had greater regret for the weight to my family.

The facade was elaborate. At seventeen, I joined the Army searching for a way to escape the churn of my own mediocrity and the path I had created in my teens. That decision paved a way to earn some stripes and badges that would disprove any allegation that I was less than a man. And so, much in the way of Red Badge of Courage, I sought the one identifier that I coveted most: the affirmation from others.

Oddly, as my military career progressed, I struggled even more to hide a truth about me and what I knew shaped me. How horrible would it be to let the fabric tear with the facts of how I failed? It simply had to be a secret. A secret that the perpetrator allured me to keep, and a secret that if shared with others would certainly ruin me. The distance between the person I was and the person I dressed up to be in uniform grew over a number of years. I struggled, but did not struggle enough to wrestle with the truth. Instead, I used the uniform and my ascension to flag rank to cover my heart, to protect my hurts, and preserve a reputation I had built. When those feelings were too hard to accept, I dulled myself with bottles of wine and isolation. But I knew the lies I lived. And I felt more guilt for not being authentic and honest with who I really was. I had not been honest with myself for too long.

I had fallen short of my own need to get rewards or recognition to cover the cracks inherent to this violation of my innocence.

The death that I sought was one of peace and quiet dignity. During an Army tour where I had an office in the Pentagon and at nearby Fort Myer, I grew an affection and great attachment to Arlington National Cemetery. This is our national cemetery where more than 400,000 heroes are buried. Each day, with precision, soldiers formed to carry the casket, sometimes with horses, to a gravesite in a field of heroes. They carried them in the rain, in the cold of winter, and at a pace that numbed me to the tragedy of death. In fact, I became enamored with the regal departure and Military Funeral Honors so well marched by the Old Guard. This milestone in death, at least from my vantage point, brought a salute and erased any harm or indignity to the individual.

For almost a year, I lived outside the gate and worked at Fort Myer where the soldiers of the Old Guard were stationed. I visited Arlington often, sometimes watching the guards change and sometimes witnessing the graveside ceremony that was replicated hundreds of times a year. The flag-covered casket carried with precision and, once set to rest, a standard script of words confirming the honor and sacrifice of the deceased. The solo Taps played, a punctuation mark on a sentence that brought both rest and gratitude. Kneeling before the family, a folded flag was presented "on behalf of a grateful nation..."

I longed for this tribute and a way to end the shame I had for failures in my own life. In this death, and with this ceremony, all would be erased for solitude. So many souls were buried at Arlington, a resting place after war and the trials of life that let them expire. I had tried, perhaps too hard, to avoid being spoiled by cracks and consequences. But the damage infected me and was central to how I understood myself.

I sought a peace that I imagined followed the somber path of the caisson, drawn by six horses pulling the casket to a resting spot. There would be one riderless horse, precisely adorned in the finest tack. And the others would have well-prepared soldiers finely executing the duties of the funeral party. This was a cloudy but calm vision to me, one that seemed so near and so much better than the torment. The vision of my funeral and the expectations I had for its dignity covered what I knew would be a painful and immediate death by suicide.

For too long I had thought of death and the way I might go. It was a tumultuous fury of ideas that haunted me. In each previous nightmare, I had somehow stepped back from the decision to go. And with each retreat I regretted it more that I lacked even the stamina to close the curtain. The handgun was in the nightstand, checked nightly by habit.

I wanted a different death. I needed to take more control of the means of my death to achieve an objective. It was to remove the wolf as the author of my end. It was okay to vanish, I thought, but it would have to be on my own and not in response to this scary figure and the persistent chase to show my fragility. In my terms, my end should bring more solace: an end to the shadow he cast on my life and an escape from a truth I could never resolve. The hollow walls of my own secret confinement made me dull and desperate.

My apartment was a convenient commute to Fort Meade, Maryland, where I had been called to active duty to lead a highly trained group of cyber security professionals for the Army. The mission too was complete with its own set of credentials and requirements for what information could not be shared. Another layer of secrets. In fact, part of the entrance criteria was to sit through a polygraph examination to certify our ability to properly work with classified material. It was a gate required for the mission and indicative of the sophisticated means to validate our senses and integrity.

Still staring out the window, I deciphered that the breath was coming from Tom, a man who touched me and tormented me for seven years of my life. Sober and awoken by a horrible dream, I felt his breath and smelled the liquor that must have drawn him to such depravity. The discovery of him as a central source of pain leading to my own sense of despair. I saw the layers of deceit in keeping the truth from all those that knew me. I saw the years that the charade had continued, a family friend who struck a relationship with a boy. I saw the numerous weekends where he picked me up, an uneven pattern that continued until I was thirteen. I felt the full weight of regret, ruin, and self-hate. I peeled away the layers of everything I had done to cover this ugliness and blamed myself for being susceptible and carrying on.

But I knew now. I knew that the pain of his abuse and the tears of a six-year-old boy were felt next to the window in Maryland. It all came together in a way I had never seen before. It was not comforting to have this insight. Even so, I did see the picture clearer and began to see my own path away from covering my hurt and into healing.

I could still see the shining parking lot, wet with rain and hidden behind a fog in the window where I leaned for support. My breath was slowing now, allowing it to cause condensation that beaded on the glass. I stared at the raindrop forming in front of me and saw the colors move in the lens made by the curved water drop. I looked intently to see the drop move slightly when other moisture added to its weight. A clearer line unevenly ran through the fogged glass. I focused now to see the lights through this one thin pane.

Unresolved, I leaned into the window and wished I felt differently in that moment. I wished for comfort and an ability to feel safe. I thought of what I might do to change the panic that covered me and shook me from rest. I thought of music and how I had been drawn into its spell. If I could find the right lyric or voice, the fear would get better and I could rest. If I could find that right melody or instrumental, I would be drawn from my darkness into a brighter place.

I remembered the times when the call of death had swarmed me, when I stood near the edge leaning into a cloudy space. My feet seemed perilously close and I felt a draft from the cliff I imagined that led to the place to die. With a fear of heights, I could not look over the edge, but nonetheless knew the moment brought me, again, to an ending place where I believed the pain would end and the only challenge was taking the next step into eternity. As clearly as I pictured that place, a thin thread tied my feet to the ground.

Closing my eyes fully, I thought of the soldiers carrying my casket, imagining how they would lift it from the hearse and turn with precision. Their steps, even over uneven ground, would lead them to the open grave dug for me. I envisioned the chaplain offering his brief scripture reading and prayer. I saw the band begin without pause playing music as the flag was folded by the guards. Triangles and stripes moved from the first soldier to the last. I could hear the distant sound of Taps playing its somber chorus while no one moved. I heard three volleys of shots from rifles offering a final salute. And I imagined for a moment that I was in the casket, in dress uniform, deceased but fully aware and looking upward.

As each person passed the casket, I wished for peace and only hoped they would one day forgive. I knew they would discover portions of me after my death and wished their sadness would not lead to anger. I imagined being able to see each one gathered around that moment, trying to reconcile and comfort. Friends and people from work. Many to support my family without question. And old friends, people from other assignments and experiences. Some placed a flower, some paused, and others touched the cold wooden casket.

Looking up from the casket, I saw each one pass, and they were faceless without identity. I saw the flowers and could smell the aroma of fresh bloom. The soldiers passed by too, and my focus was changed slightly, allowing me to see a dark face and outline. He leaned to the casket, taking a breath to gain strength, and looked deep into my eyes. It seemed I knew this figure and struggled to recognize the outline. His hand reached to me quickly, not to shake my hand. He bent closer to me and whispered, "on me." I was powerless to resist his command, and seeing him firmly clasp my wrist, his strong dark hands wrapped around me and squeezed with all his might. My vision from the prone position in the casket stopped.

Resigned, I moved to the bed where I had been unmoved and dormant for days. Migraines had sidelined my activity and likely fueled my thoughts of endings to escape the unsolvable puzzle. It would not be today that I died. I was unsure exactly why except that the dark cloud seemed to cover me less. Walking to the nearby bed, I fell into the sheets exhausted.

Searching for songs on the iPad while hiding in blankets proved fruitless. I scrolled for instrumentals frustrated I could not find something to cover a wound. Videos and links all appeared dull and wrong for the moment. And then a finer truth was revealed to me that gave me words for a poem.

THERE IS NO SONG

I can never write a song about the hands
They are with me always but are not in verse
In my life since I was too young
It's never a song, it's something worse

A chorus would be another instance
Of the times hands wrapped around me
A refrain against my will that reminds me
No song should be sung to haunt me

Fingers like these don't fit into music
Nothing lyrical in doing such wrong
Something ironic in now wanting hands to hold
Presenting the perpetually unsolved mystery
of how hands have hurt, but my heart must heal

There is injustice in never speaking the words
Or telling the story of the hands and what they took from me
I have covered the hurts with so many things
And feared that my hands too would stray

No, there are no songs about those hands
There are only these stanzas to bring to light
How a young boy felt when he touched me first
How the guilt over so many years has remained secret

It's hard to count the things ruined or infected by those years
Tears shed wanting it never to happen
Time spent wondering if the scars show
Don't take away the daily reminder that it did

Hands of injustice move my clothes and make me
They touch inside even while outside and they stain me
Hands persist and are unknown to many
And in my song, I sing alone

There could be no interlude for voice
No chorus or verse to make the hands not ruin
But for another, the music may stir a response
A trust and fellowship in a shared misfortune

How many years must a man consider these hands
When will he grow beyond the first touch of injustice

When can he forget clothes pulled away
Or must he be reminded and never let it go

What more can that abuse infect
How many bottles were spent trying to protect
And years later to be sober and reflect
That no song about hands would ever be complete

For life's circumstance must not always fit to verse
There cannot be dance for tears and worse
Hands made me bare before I knew
And I have wished for sharing, perhaps with you

Could you understand the hands that tore into my innocence?
Can I trust you to not cast doubt on each occurrence?
Could you ever know the hurt that still resides?
And makes me search for a song

CHAPTER 2

Pajamas Don't Fit

DESIGNING CLOTHES WAS NEVER HER specialty. My mom bought the patterns from the store with no focus on fashion and only the need for utility. She bought material that included a color that she liked, but she selected it because it was on sale. She was blind to what was in style. Her frugality was matched by her dedication to make clothes for herself that served a purpose, a principle she used to benefit us for many years.

One dress pattern she used most was based on the concept that a larger piece of material could have three holes for arms. The design allowed one arm to go in and then wrap the dress around so the third hole served to secure the dress when it came back to the first arm. My mother made three of these, a staple outfit for the summer when she was more active and the weather was warm. Each one had a pocket for Kleenex in front, a necessity given her asthma and allergies. The dresses were not attractive, but that was of little consequence because the dress became her routine summer outfit.

Sewing skills were translated to my older sister, enabling her to make a number of outfits for school. She was tireless in her ability to resolve small knots, misaligned seams, and the troubleshooting required for a poorly operating sewing machine. She searched for the best pattern to make a prom dress for high school and modified it as needed to make it fit her small frame. My sister Laura gleaned the essential sewing skills from my mother and then increased the use through her own hard work.

One of Mom's sewing activities was to make items for the kids. For a summer vacation, she sewed bags that could hold our sleeping bags and were cinched with a string. She made smaller bags that were a surprise when we left for vacation that had plastic toys inside. Her craft always served a great purpose and required her extra effort to complete the project within the small amount of remaining time each day. Oddly, my father never appreciated the sewing. In fact, he was irritated if the machine and all the supporting accessories were still on the dining table when he returned from work. This constraint limited the bandwidth for Mom, and somehow fueled her ability to create these items in secret.

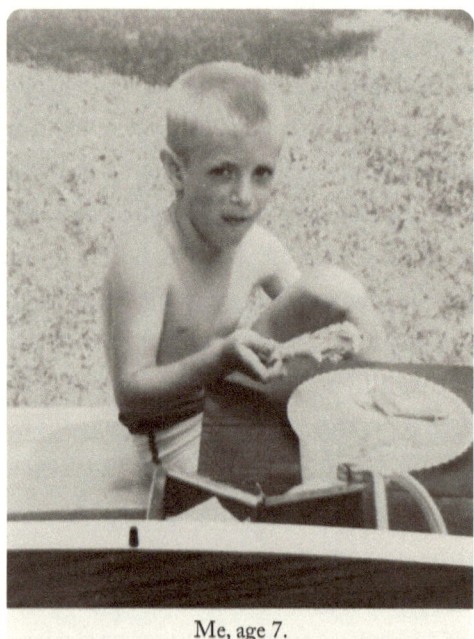

Me, age 7.

For Christmas, there were many years when Mom made pajamas for all the kids. One pattern served four children as she simply estimated smaller sizes after cutting the first. Her approach translated to pajamas that we wore without addressing any inaccuracy. At some level, we knew the challenge she faced in getting any sewing done with Dad's dining table prohibition. Every evening the table must be clear for dinner; no folded clothes, kids' homework, or sewing. So, it was equally as remarkable that she produced four sets of pajamas in such short order and without any of the recipients being the wiser. With a Christmas tree that had few wrapped gifts underneath, the pajamas were a warm and welcome gift that highlighted Mom's behind-the-scenes care and generous heart.

Dad had his own additional list of prohibitions for the house that included the shop he fashioned from leftover lumber in our garage. This is where he hung his tools so they would never be touched. The floor was made from leftover parquet flooring from a construction project from his work. The garage itself was nothing special, but if you looked into the corner, you could see a well-organized shop with tools neatly hung and an excellent parquet floor. A bright fluorescent light hovered over the saw, bench, and tools. On weekends he could disappear into this space to troubleshoot something or use a radial arm saw to cut wood. Frequently the radio played Chicago Cubs baseball, and he listened intently and privately to his team while completing his work. The shop was his private place, so special that he soon built a rolling door that included a hanging latch so it would be closed.

Every boy seems naturally led to tools and the exploration of how things work. This was certainly true for me, taking great notice of Dad's shop, and sitting on the steps looking into his space when the door was open. There were times when I was drafted to assist, a requirement that came with a quick verbal blast and directions on exactly what to do. Holding tools or shining a light became ways to participate, to see the craftsman and feel fortunate to help, albeit with reprimands when the assistance fell short.

On a December afternoon, the allure of the door and all the shop's contents became a curiosity I could no longer resist. I walked by it closely at first while tending to the trash can, doing my required chore. But then I stopped to look in, and it was too dark to see the contents or project that was neatly set on the bench. The latch to the door was a metal hook, a simple element that could be opened without any traceable evidence. I pressed into the door and it rolled slightly. And then more. On an impulse, I saw the latch and without hesitation lifted it to allow the door to open further. As the view into the space increased, I saw the large blue blanket covering something in the middle of the shop. I inhaled to take in the fresh smell of pine sawdust, remnants of Dad's most recent project.

Knowing I had crossed a dangerous line, I slid the door closed again and looked back to the side entrance of the house. Has my path been seen? With no evidence that my exploration was noticed, I moved the door open again, except now I was ever more careful to make no noise and offer no hints of my potential discovery. The blue blanket covered boxes that were stacked at a height above my waist. With only one step I could reach the blanket, a distance that seemed too close to challenge. As I reached for the blanket, it lifted easily and the colored box was visible from the side. Immediately I recognized the Fisher-Price logo and saw the words, "Kids Car Garage."

Surprise and excitement covered my apprehensions and brought a smile to me. Immensely satisfied with the discovery, I untraced my route and lifted up to take a step back to close the door. And then Mom's words rang out as the house door opened, "Did you get the new trash bag?" My escape quickened and the door slid closed while I reached for the latch. She turned the garage light on. My hand had just left the metal when the door was fully open and she saw me standing directly in front of the door. Of the shop. The off-limits shop. The shop that stored items not to be seen. That I had just seen.

Sullen and drawn to tears, I came to the door blending words of apology for seeing the shop while explaining my detour from the trash can. As I entered the house, she bent slightly to speak to me, reiterating that the shop was not a place for me to be. And then her arm touched my shoulder as she asked, "Did you see?" Her inquiry jumped straight to the point, avoiding my excuses or reasoning. "Did you look inside the shop? Did you look?" Her repetition fueled my tears and made me look down in shame.

"What would happen if you ruined your own Christmas?" This question, however rhetorical, had not crossed my mind, but the discovery definitely unveiled the one gift intended for me. In telling me that I should not have looked, she softly scolded me again. "You can't tell this secret, can you?" hinting that I might share the news with my sister and also spoil her surprise. No, I shook my head, I cannot tell. And somehow this provided a calm turning point to her correcting my disobedience. The burden was now mine to carry the un-story forward and ensure that our family gift opening was not spoiled by my eyes or confession.

Fall weekends included the Saturday evening bowling league, a recurring date that drew my parents away and allowed our bed time to lapse until 9 p.m. This was time enough for evening variety shows and room enough for Laura, my sister six years older, to watch over her younger siblings. She did so with such grace and was the warm caregiver that made a milkshake or evening dessert. Although interested in the television, frequently this was a sewing space as well and a time to prepare a new outfit. Stitching together under a dim light from the machine, she focused intently, pausing occasionally to check on us.

The league was mostly drafted from the adults from the local catholic church, many of whom were founders to the parish in the small suburb of Streamwood, Illinois. Although there were scores and competition, the emphasis was on the interaction, a lively time to drink together oddly paired with their likely intersection the following morning at church. They were tied together, as were their families and the routine that allowed them an evening out.

In the informal tribe of families that belonged to the church that went camping together and gathered together, there were two middle-aged men. These two had been adopted from work relationships and quickly grew in esteem from the group, particularly because one took an interest in the teens and was a good sport for jokes and interaction. Each volunteered their car and participation to allow the kids to practice driving. They joked around with the teens and were willing to be teased, unlike our serious parents. Soon they had nicknames and were accepted as uncles to the kids with an open invite to any gathering and home. Tom was the younger, a subordinate to one of the parents at work who was invited for dinner and adopted into the family. He was overweight, high performing at work, and quiet about his service in the Marine Corps during the Vietnam era.

Tom didn't bowl with the group but would occasionally share a portion of that evening with adults. When Mom asked him for dinner before they left for their Saturday evening ritual, he gladly accepted and stayed when they departed. He too, so he said, loved the Carole Burnett show and knew how to make a milkshake. In fact, he had a special recipe, and therein created his premise for being in our home with three kids under the age of fourteen.

Laura was fastidious in her crafting of a dress, a new pattern that drew her full attention. When the dishes were done and the table cleared, she positioned herself with the sewing machine and used the desk lamp to see her work. The shows were tuned on our nineteen-inch black-and-white TV, and this Saturday appeared like every other in bowling season.

Jokes and teasing were organic to exchanges with Tom, his slight criticisms or challenges were funny and created for laughter. I was alone at the table when he sat next to me, chiding me about my pajamas and how they did not fit. I was quick to defend the seamstress and my mother's effort and her perennial homemade gift. He pointed to the button that was loose. He jabbed with his finger at the armpit trying to induce tickling. His effort worked and I wiggled and twisted to avoid the touch. He persisted, but had now turned his attention to the waist tie string that was worn and not secure. I saw the aimpoint and countered by grabbing the waist to pull it up. And then the tickle pokes went to my sides and stomach. My hand moved from the waist and the pajama bottoms seemed even more loose. With speedy hands, I secured the bottoms and prevented them from falling. And then the challenge began.

"Can you trust me and just hold your hands up for ten seconds?" It was a game created to keep me from securing the pajamas when the tickles became touches. "You're terrible at this. Do you trust me for five seconds?" And suddenly he saw my tears and knew I hated the game, its challenge, and the idea that my pants would fall down. Quickly shifting, Tom chided, "You'd better not cry or your sister will see you and think you are a baby." He leaned in to correct me, his bourbon breath and cigar smell becoming clearer. I attempted to quiet my tears with one hand desperately holding my pajamas and the other wiping my face.

Seeing that the quiet pursuit may get louder with my crying, he said, "You're so tired, you need to get to bed." With that declaration we moved to my room and his conversation shifted to how I had ruined the pajamas. "Does your mother know that you ripped them?" I hadn't ripped them, except Tom saw they no longer held to my waist and attributed the error to me. Another round of "hold your hands up" ensued, this time to see if he could fix them. His face was close to my chest. Sequestered in the small room I shared with my brother, away for the evening, I raised my hands, almost surrendering to the prosecution of the ruined pajamas that kept falling down. My mother, he hinted, "would be so disappointed that the gift she gave was in such bad shape." And so, she must never know. The failure of the waistband after more than a year's use was not the culprit, it was my dereliction instead. I could not bear letting her know. Anything.

As quickly as I tried to rescue the bottoms from falling down, there was another movement in the loop my mind had woven. The narrative of my failure and shame for ruining the pajamas picked up pace. She would be so devastated to have her gift disrespected, and my shame for letting my pants fall would never go away. And then my hands were raised higher, the underwear slid slowly, and with each movement the hands adjusted.

Suppressing my tears, I closed my eyes slightly, feeling the weight of the teardrop in my lashes before it fell. I stared into the corner, keeping pace with the directions and feeling heat cover me like guilt that dripped. Mom can never find out, a premise that provided fuel. Through a squint, I focused on my brother's acoustic guitar and wished for the song he might play. The guitar changed shape with a tear to obstruct my clear sight, and my face felt the contrast of cold as moisture covered my cheeks. I cried silently. I moved slowly. I centered on the guitar music I hoped for in the lonely space of the small room. The touches continued. Through the squint of my eye, I looked again at the guitar, slightly opening and closing my eyes in repetition. Hands moved my body, but my sight of the acoustic was more attune. I squinted more tightly and the scene went to black and white. There was brilliance and changing shapes. Tears that rolled down my face streamed together and I consolidated my thoughts to the instrument that, like me, remained silent and unheard.

(Author's Note: From the age of six until thirteen, there were continued intersections and moments where I was alone with Tom. His endorsement as a family member endured and actually was given increased credibility when he moved to Wisconsin. From that time forward, he made return trips to Streamwood to visit.)

When neighbors decided their silver artificial Christmas tree was no longer of use, we inherited it and used it as a second tree placed in our small living room. It was a shaggy tree by now and made from wire branches covered with silver tinsel. With lights and ornaments, so we believed, almost any tree would shine and add to our limited Christmas decorations. Our tradition was to have a real tree at the back of the house that was not put up until Christmas morning. Santa had the duty of taking the tree from the garage, placing it on a stand, adding lights and ornaments and eventually gifts before the kids woke up. This would have been complex, but was even more challenging as we attended Midnight Mass on Christmas Eve. That reality whittled the time for the entire evolution and likely explained my parents' afternoon nap on Christmas day.

The silver tree had all the ornaments that were handmade by the kids and included the older and larger set of Christmas lights. The bulbs were bigger and the lights were fewer, but it fit into our desire to see decorations earlier and welcome the season. The lights were near the front window and emitted heat that caused moisture to form on the glass panes.

Looking from the window, I stared into the driveway looking over the bright bulbs and seeing the moisture form droplets. I moved closer and my breath aimed in the direction of the glass added to the moisture. Oddly, I waited for Tom to arrive knowing he would pull into the driveway soon for the weekend trip he had planned. Only moments before I had been corrected by Mom and told to wait in the living room.

"You have a chance to be away and do something nice in Wisconsin," she began, seeing that I was dull to the prospect of leaving. "Pack your things and be grateful. How many kids get to go on a special trip?" And then the list of potential activities was part of the critique. Breakfast at the pancake house, pizza for dinner, and a chance to see semi-trucks where he worked. My mind had not considered the activities and instead felt the guilt of knowing it was different. "You show him that you are grateful" was the last direction before I stood in the living room with the small bag she had sewn for me with two days of clothes. I held grateful. I held the secret, too.

Looking above the bulb, there was darkness in the street but enough light to see our driveway. I saw other passing cars and was grateful for each one. Anxious about leaving and wondering what ruse would allow touches for this visit, my emotions swelled, as did tears. The light formed a prism and the silver tree and big bulbs offered a colorful array of shapes and colors. Sighing, I closed my eyes very slowly and concentrated on the spectrum and design. Red and bright orange moved together and white shimmered from the silver tree. Looking forward, I saw the reflection of my face and the dripping window pane. My ears rang while I squinted tighter, changing the bright colors to black and white. I exhaled more deeply into the window and saw two drops collide when his car pulled into the driveway.

Heat from my own thoughts and intense feelings allowed me to go out the front door without a goodbye and into a cold night before opening his car door. The smell of cigar smoke poured out as I slid into the Oldsmobile Cutlas, a sportier car choice for the bachelor everyone adored. Burgundy paint was contrasted with a cream-colored vinyl roof. The interior paired the cream color and the eight-track tape deck and music system were upgrades to the stock adornments.

Miles to Racine, Wisconsin, passed by slowly with accompaniment from the music and a recurring set of questions. The inquiry about school turned into a warning about doing well. The questions about friends were a query about who you should trust. Asking about sports was an opportunity to grade my physicality and whether I was strong enough. Each placed a level of doubt on my emerging sense of who I was and struggle to become me. My appearance, a young boy with bad haircuts from my father, was a chance to tease and challenge. In each area I found truth and a basis for criticism. Tom's response was to suggest that these deficits would require work. But more, each of them was faults that others would mock.

Tom presented as the arbiter of each facet of my person and how it ranked on a scale. Few were seen as normal and all required fixes. An older man, he shared, knew about what girls were looking for and it was such a shame that I fell short. He could help. He could show me how to get strong. "Muscles," he said touching my arm, "grow when you work them. I can show you that." Pimples too were something to fear and Tom knew how to wash my face. Posture was a leading way to show confidence, and Tom knew how to help me stand up straight.

Arriving at his apartment, the allure of a candy bar drew me into his space and spell. In the hours ahead, each of the topics of my attributes received attention, some requiring physical inspection. How disappointed he was that I was falling short in these areas. What would kids at school say if they knew? They will tease you and never let you be a friend if you are not strong, have zits, or don't have confidence. Why were my arms soft? Why was my stomach soft? Why weren't my legs strong like other boys? There was no object to stare into as the inspection continued. Clothes were moved because it was time for bed. But I could not wear the pajamas, how silly I forgot that they did not fit. You wear your underwear.

But underwear wouldn't do. He had a t-shirt that I should wear. The idea did not register with me, but I considered the coverage from a shirt to be an advantage. Yes, I would wear his t-shirt. And then the rule changed. If you wear a t-shirt, then you don't wear underwear.

Wearing only the t-shirt felt unnatural and naked to me. I didn't want the exposure and was sad seeing him put my clothes in his closet. Uncomfortable in my appointed outfit, I crawled under the covers, doubling my yawn and imitating my very best tired display.

Tom saw through the charade and told me I should not sleep in that position. No, I had to turn that way. And the tickles. But I should be still. My legs had to be apart like this. And tickles. And my tears. And a loud voice not to be such a baby. My parents had asked him to take me to have a good time, but now I was ruining it. Wouldn't they be mad? Wouldn't they be disappointed in me? I should be grateful. If I was, he would not tell them. They would not know our secret.

My ears were ringing and I was too warm under the sheets. The tears made the pillow moist and I tried to inhale and make the crying stop with an exhale. My stomach hurt and I felt so exposed in the t-shirt. Nothing fits, not pajamas and now t-shirts.

Morning sun peeked through the upstairs bedroom and I awoke cold without a cover. I moved quickly to see my pants on the floor in the closet and aimed at them exiting the bed. His plea for me to return caught me as I was at the bathroom door. A stack of Playboy magazines was next to the stool. Ashes were around the sink with matches to light cigars. I reached for the pants when he called out to leave the door open while I peed. Taking a breath in front of the toilet, I remembered the promise of pancakes and considered what it would take to get there.

Waiting in the crowded lobby, we stood along the wall for our table. The clanking of dishes and smell of coffee covered the space. Names were called but we waited still, testing my endurance and hunger for pancakes. I told Tom I needed to use the bathroom and he said he would show me where they were since it was crowded.

Stepping from the lobby, I looked ahead, seeing the sign with him behind me, guiding my shoulder. We passed people and navigated near the space when he opened the door. His hand became more firm on my shoulder and he pushed me into the room. The door closed quickly and I immediately smelled perfume.

Seeing the stall open, a young woman continued to pull her pants up and gasped discovering a boy in the women's bathroom. I stepped backward and felt my stomach twinge and fear cover me. I leaned into the door, but it seemed stuck and would not open. I turned and pushed harder. "You get out of here!" the woman yelled, and I hoped to escape before she completed the sentence.

I pushed again on the door exerting even more force. It opened slightly and then slammed shut. I leaned forward and pushed with all my strength. The door opened just a little and then closed, and then my effort pushed it further. Tom was on the other side wedging his foot and shoulder to keep the door closed. When he stepped away, I rushed forward, nearly falling as the door flung wide open. The air from the restaurant rushed to my face as I inhaled the view people had of a boy leaving the women's bathroom. Shame covered me.

His sly smile was mixed with his chiding voice asking me what I was doing in the girl's bathroom. What were you doing? What did you see in there? Were you trying to be naughty? Don't you know you will get in trouble? What if they told the restaurant manager? What if I got caught? I really should be ashamed. His devilish grin persisted and the tears welled up in my eyes, taking away thoughts of pancakes.

Tom sat for breakfast with the smirk of a conqueror having succeeded with the bathroom prank and savoring my compromise. He ordered his breakfast and paused between bites to comment on the waitress and challenge my interest. Shaken by the storm and embarrassment, I considered how little impact having three syrup choices were in making me happy given the way my stomach knotted.

Over the next seven years, there were numerous intersections with Tom. My struggle to understand myself grew tighter in focus with each overlap. The scrutiny was paired with the torment. The requirement to keep these faults hidden was endorsed by him. And his professed ability to fix them added to his ironic credibility. In fact, I needed his involvement and formula for repair.

CHAPTER 3

The Next Grade

SITTING AT THE WINDOW, I looked out to the smaller playground at Woodland Heights, the elementary school that was a twelve-minute walk from my house. Having heard the bell ring with sounds of children that exited the building, I saw the place was empty now. A half-day schedule cut the day short. The fight I got into with Scotty Lefler took me from the classroom and into this small space after my punishment.

Collins was a tall woman, a white-haired older lady who had parked her mannerisms and approach to life in the late fifties. She had set on a steady course and stayed there. Her clothes matched that era. She was a traditional person; a stoic whose lessons were delivered in the same way each day. She was stern and leveraged her physique and grandmotherly persona to influence her students. Given her decades of experience in the classroom, she could spot disobedience at a distance. She had mastered third grade some time ago and now stood in front of us as an unmovable character, part of the fabric of Woodland Heights.

Her approach left little room for derivation from the prescribed path. She was particularly committed to cursive writing, a focal point during the first part of the year. She had no appreciation for student weaknesses. Mine was handwriting. Barely able to letter in the proper form, my left-handed letters were tilted, uneven, and a source of criticism from Collins. She had taken the time to scribe her appraisal in the first grade report. More worksheets were required for me in order to follow the template and learn cursive.

"You're wasting time writing like that," taking the moment to touch my left hand. I knew the letters were sloppy and was tuned into the way my lack of ability in this area missed her expectations. With a rubber eraser covering the pencil to make it easier to hold, she expected there would be improvement. My letters never improved, leaving me outside of her approval circle, reflected in the last poor grades leading to fourth grade.

Rust was an equally tall but younger version of Collins. She earned the reputation, certainly by her name, as a metallic figure who taught the fourth grade. In addition to her stern approach, she had the ability to raise her voice mimicking the anger and condemnation that came from parents. The outbursts were frequent enough to disturb our trust in the teacher. There was irony in her ability to play piano, a gift she shared during afternoon music and song singing. How could it be that a mean lady played the singalong songs?

Thirty children were a lot to have in a classroom, especially at those busy ages. Rust leveraged her screeching voice and fear to direct, correct, and shape student behaviors. Her tactical approach left little room for shenanigans and chatter. Her class, much like third grade with Collins, was rigid and focused on the delivery she knew and would not stray from.

The Pledge of Allegiance, a given part of the morning sequence, began promptly after the eight o'clock bell. We stood by our desks and faced the flag at the front of the room, repeating the pledge as we had been taught from the beginning. Once complete, her agenda began with writing and English, and the day unfolded as a predictable routine.

Scotty Lefler sat to my right in desks that were arranged in neat rows and columns. He was a bratty boy, shorter than most of the class and plagued with a bad attitude and insistence that he was funny and deserved attention. His antics were not understood, somehow fueling his need to be recognized.

When the pledge was complete, I lowered myself to the seat and felt a sharp stab into my right butt cheek. Already doubled over in laughter, Scotty was kneeling next to my desk, having created a way to make me sit on his sharp pencil. My quick outbursts of pain were heard by other kids around me, but Lefler's giddy laughter was even louder. Without noticing, Rust moved to the door, stepping from the classroom before the commotion came to her attention.

Warm blood oozed down my leg and tears came to me as I tried to sit at the desk. But Scotty had finally invented a prank that drew attention and made others laugh, too. Their exclamation and giggling joined his, and soon the class of kids saw his achievement, a piercing and classic sharp pencil trick that hurt and preyed upon the fool. I felt warmth flush to my face. My tears stopped. Rage filled me. I turned to glare at him. Scotty's face and celebration appeared in slow motion as my anger spilled over.

Stepping to his desk, I quickly pushed him, causing him to step back and draw his arms up with the pencil weapon still in his tight grip. I grabbed the arm with the pencil to stop its second effort motion and wrapped my arms around him when he spun to elude me. With a bear hug, I lifted him from the ground feeling some satisfaction that I had captured the monster. Rust burst through the door. The yelling from the kids came to a halt. In the silence that had instantly replaced the cheering, she saw me holding on to Scotty, my face red and the desks ajar from our fracas.

"You! Out!" was her only command, given with a pointed finger for the classroom door. I marched slowly forward knowing I had been convicted, sent to the hall with an unknown term or outcome. "Right there!" and her finger pointed to the hallway bench located under the coat hooks that lined the hallway. I sat slowly, feeling the pain of the wound and resigned to the trouble I was in for grabbing Scotty.

Without inquiry or question, Rust sent me to the principal's office, a sentence that peaked the list of terrible things that could be done to boys who misbehave. The principal was an imposing figure, perhaps as much for his authority as his blank and emotionless composition. Standing in front of his desk, his thin face was expressionless while explaining that I was to be punished for causing a classroom fight. Two whacks from the paddle was his prescription, and reaching into his desk drawer, he quickly drew the weapon and stood to approach me. His tall frame moved from his seat next to me in front of his desk.

He began speaking, giving me directions on how the spanking would be administered. He pushed me to the front of his desk and my hands grabbed the front, conforming to the bent over position he wanted. Fear covered me as I considered how quickly the morning had changed when I was pierced by a pencil and drawn to such anger. The sounds of laughter and Scotty's contorted face in his success made it clear that Adam was the source of entertainment, a fool whose injury proved funny.

His hands grabbed my belt, pulling my waist backward to make it easier to strike with the paddle. I lifted my head from the desk, looking forward into a cabinet. I focused intently on the drawer and the metal handle. I looked at the clasp, and with every detail turned myself from the room where I stood bent over to another place I imagined. His hand moved at my belt, persuading my position and stirring me to tune further into the cabinet and clasp. My mind explored every facet of the cabinet, each detail and its steady and immovable position. Focused on the metal-formed handle, I closed my eyes slightly and felt my body jolt forward with the first strike. Feeling tears from the pain, I felt my pants pull away from the skin and the dried blood from Scotty's successful prank. With the second paddle, I moved farther still, now bent over the desk, save for my head, completely locked and intensely staring at the metal cabinet.

His directions after the punishment were simple: sit in the room adjacent to his office and wait. The doorway was in the back of his office, a small room with a table, two chairs, and a window. The light was not turned on and only shadows from outside partially lit the small space. Separated from his motions, I moved to the window and felt the sadness sweep over me again. I felt the injustice of the moment, how I had been punished when Scotty initiated the event with no consequence. I considered what might be next and thought of the shame of my parents. Looking at the playground, I felt the guilt of knowing I was in trouble and considering the additional layers that would be added at home. A boy, kicked out of school.

Sitting at the table, I took the moments to finally cry and put my hands into my arms folded at the table. Quietly sobbing, I took inventory of the event and saw the ridicule that so easily came from others. And why me? What did Scotty see in Adam that made me the target of his scheme? What did he know? Was I an easier target and someone he knew would fall to his pencil trick? I imagined his grinning face and saw the victory he savored for finally crafting a way to make another person the stooge. And that fool was me.

The sidewalk leading to school was a simple left turn from our front door. Uneven and broken, I took pride in walking in a way that avoided stepping onto the cracks. I considered this a personal hobby, one that I translated inside Woodland Heights where I learned to avoid cracks between floor tiles and in the pavement leading to the door.

As I exited the school, I considered the walk home to my awaiting mother, hoping to avoid even more cracks in an effort to decrease the severity of her response. It didn't work out that way. Her first question asked why I was late coming home. And, in an impulsive move, I actually told her the truth, not knowing that the principal had called minutes prior to give her an update before my arrival. And then he too was honest, and he apologized that he forgot I was in the adjacent office alone after the paddling.

Her tears were first, and then her anger saying, "you're putting your brains under a rock." Devastated that I had caused her more stress and disappointment, I listened intently. She was there to see me leave in the morning for school and always had lunch made when I came home mid-day. She was dedicated to my school and learning, suggesting she would have been more grateful when she was growing up. Her father had died before she was one year old, and the Depression-era answer to these losses for widows was to ask relatives to raise the child. So her mother returned to work, she lived in Michigan with grandparents, and her schooling took second place among chores. The lesson stung me even without her raising a voice.

The second and perhaps more complex obstacle was letting Dad know. His return from work only varied by minutes each day, giving Mom adequate time to make sure dinner was nearly done. She had time to clear any clutter from the kitchen table of any remnants from laundry or projects during the day. Once he came through the door, he made quick work of changing from work shoes to slippers, a habit he remained committed to no matter the season. Slippers were my frequent chore, and tonight I was especially sure to have them near the door. Cocktails were served before dinner from the bar that was installed in a small family room. He lit a cigarette, offered quick commentary on the day and prepared for dinner. When Mom wanted additional time for dinner, she brought the Velveeta cheese to the bar with crackers, allowing a quick few slices to keep his hunger at bay. She had the crackers on the plate along with the cheese she had already sliced. Dinner could wait.

Demonstrating her ability to protect, Mom shared the news first and began with her disappointment that the principal called to apologize. The way she prioritized that headline had everything to do with his reaction. Imagining what he would have liked to say if he had answered the call, he began to improvise lines. "Just what in the hell are you doing in that school?" he barked. And then criticizing him for forgetting, "maybe I should come over there and help you remember!" Her angle and approach camouflaged what had happened and led him into an unheard rant for him to create lines.

Ms. Blevins was a steady figure at Woodland Heights where she had served as the school counselor for more than a decade. She came to Rust's class the following Monday to escort me to a session with her, one of the requirements for returning to class. Blevins appeared far too kind to be the one to help boys in trouble. Her office, ironically, was the same one the principal used as a waiting space. But the lights were on now. She sat next to me at the table. There were no questions or mention of the scuffle, punishment, or what I had done wrong. She reached to a cabinet where she had an assortment of games. "Which one looks fun?" I knew none of the games, none of the counselor techniques, and was only recently familiar with the small room. We met there weekly for the remainder of the year. I never got good at pick up sticks. I wondered if she would ever ask me what was wrong.

CHAPTER 4

Campfire Songs

FOR MY OLDER BROTHER'S THIRD birthday, he got a plastic guitar. With cheap plastic strings and tuning pegs, Dad began to strum his gift to amuse his little boy. There were four strings, enough to make chords and slowly learn songs. The easiest to learn were radio jingles, quick melodies that Dad could mimic and enjoy. It was not long before it was more an instrument for Dad, a frequent outlet for entertaining even though he never learned more than four chords. Soon he increased his repertoire and sang songs even if the chords were not right. He had taught himself to play the guitar. Not well, but he played it. Except that it was plastic. Except that it only had four strings. He could not have been more encouraged.

Dad inherited a love for music from his father who sat in their small living room with neighbors to enjoy their record player. After a day of work or as a weekend delight, they played vinyl 78s, fast-moving records that were heavy and brittle. Each of the neighbors collected great recordings and in recurring sessions they played some of the new and all of their old favorites. Some were popular big band tunes or ballads from the 1940s. Others were eclectic pieces from orchestra or musical comedians.

Graduating from the plastic instrument, Dad purchased a wooden ukulele to play and tuned it like the guitar. By now he had mastered a set of songs and ditties that he and Mom sang together. With no television in their small apartment, sharing a melody and verse became a frequent pastime.

Sears was the large department and catalog store. When I was seven, we went as a family to Sears shortly after Dad received our tax refund. We went together to look at the "Sears 8," a sleeping camper on wheels that he intended to purchase. The camper was bare bones but advertised that it had room for eight to sleep. With four children and two dogs, it was an inelegant but perfect fit.

In earlier years, a tent had been the vessel for camping, traveling to nearby Indiana or Michigan for weekend trips. The tent was made of canvas and, in addition to its weight and complexity in setting up, leaked along the seams and windows. Setting up the tent was an arduous process that truly only advantaged the help of my older siblings. There was ample time for complaints and direction from Dad.

Having grown up with modest means in the Depression, Dad took pride in what he perceived as his ability to break out and make a living. The trailer camper was a symbol of this exact achievement, the ability to afford an actual Sears 8 as evidence of this status. Not everyone had a camper; actually, many were in tents that smelled like mildew because they leaked. Not everyone had a camper that could fit that many people. With the camper, our outdoor travel could really take shape using the trailer to carry additional gear. We had arrived, but only to leave and go camping.

In Dad's amazing but private shop, he constructed a cabinet that stored dishes, pans, and silverware for camping. One of his principal design objectives was sturdiness, a goal he easily achieved when the wooden box weighed almost sixty pounds. He had measured it to fit precisely inside the trailer, and it was a three-person lift to move in position to support meal preparation and eating.

The cooler was the second most important component, not because it stored food but because it kept beer cold. In optimal Dad vacation planning, days of travel began early and beer was open at 3:00 p.m.

This routine was what made camping great: early morning coffee and an earlier start to the beverages. Beer was followed by cocktails, a fire, and finally, campfire songs.

A recurring camping trip was to a state park thirty minutes outside Kalamazoo, Michigan. Although there was much that could have made this park a great choice, its proximity to the Kellogg factory was the leading factor. During these trips, the first morning after arrival we would load up and make our way to the Kellogg cereal factory to tour. In addition to seeing how amazing it was to see Frosted Flakes from start to delicious finish, each tour ended with a souvenir sample. Dad took pride in knowing this hack, that by visiting during our camping trip, he netted a week's worth of breakfast cereal. He even bragged about it to us with each visit. "You see there, we've got food to last for the trip," and with great pride, we saw his smile. Each of us looked at our assortment box of cereals and traded for the Apple Jacks.

Evenings while camping were an easy wind down after a day of swimming, exploring the woods, or maybe fishing from the shore. Dad was unlikely to be involved in the daytime activity, but he was the centerpiece of the campfire.

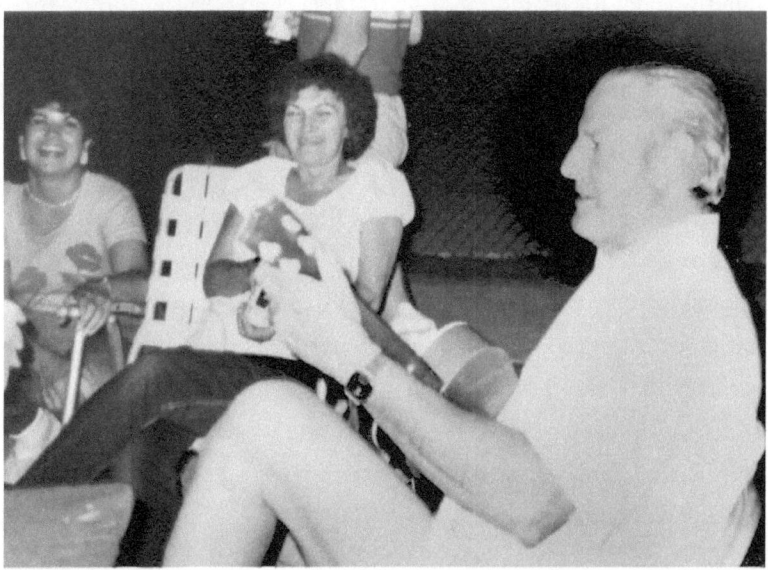

Short songs and melodies were all Dad knew and he always played in the key of G. That restriction was linked to his limited chord menu, a constraint that became a running joke when asked to play a song. "Sure, I'll play anything you want, but it'll be in G." He loved to sing old tunes and knew the first verse of too many and the entirety of few. In between songs and sips of beer, he recited a number of quips that he memorized from radio. The routine was seemingly never dated as it remained always fixed to what he knew. He enlisted my mom to join in and found opportunities to wince or comment about her terrible singing voice. His appraisal was not without basis.

The highlight of the singalong was Mom and Dad singing "There's a hole in the bucket," a silly lyrical that trades lines between two people. The chorus is the title and, in each verse, Dad would play the part of a man telling a woman there was a hole in the bucket. She replied with suggestions to fix it, and each one met with a sillier reply why that solution would not work. Eventually, and after elongated drama enjoyed in musical theater by my parents, the argument goes full circle and they both join in the chorus.

Songs and exchanges like this drew attention in a campground and it was not uncommon to have strangers join our fire, adding their chairs in a circle. What we did not have in a fancy trailer we had in entertainment. Dad adored the attention and played nearly the same repertoire of songs any time he played. He never tired of the songs and was fueled by the attention and experience.

Camping drew many of our family friends from Streamwood. They came to Indiana and we rambled around during the day enjoying our fellowship and time together. Several of them had musical abilities and this made the campfire even more robust and eclectic. One family had sixteen children and they were assigned a nightly duty to share a song or ditty. One father played the clarinet and would stand as he played the Clarinet Polka. It was all quite entertaining and was a staple of our summer camping adventures.

My brother, Joe, more than seven years older than me, played guitar and would join in the circle to share songs. He was far more musically capable than Dad and played a variety of contemporary songs. One favorite was Jim Croce's "Bad, Bad Leroy Brown," that was popular on the radio. He added his own flair to it, not with better guitar playing, but adding his own theatrical effects. He added a story of his childhood as a prelude and then slowly got into the music. Around the fire, it was a song that led to clapping along, bad (clap), bad (clap), Leroy Brown (clap), baddest man in the whole damn town (clap), meaner than a junkyard dog (clap).

The songs of summer made their way to the church singing group the "Swinging Singers." This was organized by one of the moms and quickly grew to more than eighty kids who sometimes sang in church and always sang in the church program over Labor Day weekend. Each year the growing church organized a carnival in the fall with rides and booths to raise money for the school. Each season brought new themes and musicals to showcase for the singing group. Joe played guitar along with another mom who played piano. Other friends joined who played drums, bass, and had the makings of a band. In a small suburb where the church was the centerpiece, the "Swinging Singers" were visible and enjoyed.

There was a junior group that my sister, Deb, and I were placed. One season, we sang music from the Wizard of Oz, and she was naturally amazing as the Cowardly Lion. For no known reason, I was chosen for the part of the wizard. It was awkward for me because I was younger than the other characters and somehow given the role of wise elder. A refrigerator box had been modified to look like the wizard's machine and hiding place. I enjoyed looking through its cutout windows and colored panes into the audience.

In the next season, I was assigned "Candyman," a popular song from the original Willy Wonka show. This part was equally challenging and included a solo that required a confidence I did not have. The lyrics chimed that the Candyman makes "everything he bakes satisfying and delicious." This was a claim unbefitting my youth and in contrast to my angst about this song and me. I found in each part an inability to draw from wise solutions that I had or could convey to others. At eight years old, I could not drift from my own reality and escape into a character for the sake of a song. I wanted to, especially when I knew the performance was terrible, but the belief just wasn't there.

In the neighboring town there was a home where foster children lived and stayed, a ministry of the church that housed more than thirty kids. At the suggestion of another parent, our small group of friends made their way to share songs in that home. Although the invitation was rather impromptu, we met at our home first to drive together. Some of the parents lobbied around the bar in our family room sharing a beer before we left.

The stale smell of mildew met us at the doorway. Walking through the hallway to the gathering place, dents in the walls and worn doorways were a measure of the movement inside. Sitting in a small circle of chairs were more than a dozen kids aging five to seventeen. Their eyes pierced the traveling group that invited themselves into their space. There was disbelief and sadness.

Sitting at the end of a couch, a teenage girl was dressed in layers. Too many layers. Her pants were under a dress, a sweatshirt tightly over many tee shirts, and her hat was snug to her ears. She looked away, and we arranged ourselves at the front of the room awkwardly while my brother took his guitar from the case. Mom moved next to the girl wearing all of her clothes. The clarinet moved to the side of the crowded room. Dad's ukulele was in his hand when he took center and asked if anybody wanted to sing a song. There was silence.

Standing in the front, we began a short list of songs, none better than the other but slowly seeming to warm the room. Dad backed away from the center and Joe came forward to share "Country Roads." He sat on the other edge of the couch. In the chorus, some lips actually moved. "Yes," I thought, take me to that place where I belong.

There was no finale because there was no known song order. Even so, Dad found a way to strum a few bars of "Hole in the Bucket," chiding Mom to join him and begin their routine. The best part was not the climactic chorus. The best part was the drama and banter between these two singing characters acting out their frustration that solutions for a derelict bucket were not found. They exaggerated and overplayed the part, a theatrical opportunity she used to voice a discontent with the other character that she would have never voiced in real life. It drew smiles. A song so silly and long was delivered masterfully, transforming the cloudy room into laughter.

Mom returned to the couch, now sitting a little closer to the girl with many clothes who smiled and welcomed her back to the space. Looking over to her, I saw the girl whisper in Mom's ear, a gesture that created a beaming smile from Mom who leaned into the girl and held her hand. She was a little safer, and together it appeared they could avoid any ridicule with their new alliance.

Seeing that he had finally captured the audience's imagination, Dad chose an even sillier song as he led "On Top of Spaghetti!" He shouted out the verse, leading the group to repeat it like an Army cadence. "All covered in cheese!" his voice broadcast to the group. They joined in with vigor, surrendering their dreary surroundings for a few moments of escape. Sparked by their voices, he became more animated, partly from his own joy and further fueled by beverages before departure. He blared each line, and the audience was equally as entertained by his overcharged display and musical storytelling. It would be hard for anyone to make the ukulele offer dramatic contrast or sophistication, and yet on that day, in that small dark room, he brought light.

CHAPTER 5

The Shower Is Over

ON THE UPSIDE OF A grassy hill, James and Grace moved to a home in South Carolina, the location for a new manufacturing plant where he would work. Their departure fueled the intent to travel there as part of a family vacation. In the months of planning, the dates were set by phone along with instructions on how to get there and what to bring. The new location had many advantages for the business but offered equally as many differences for social interactions and entertainment.

In the small town where they lived, the county adhered to a well appreciated legacy restriction on selling alcohol. None of the local restaurants served, and there were no taverns or places to get a drink. Purchasing alcohol was done only at state-authorized locations, none of which were located in their county or the surrounding forty miles.

Vacationing without a camper was unfamiliar to us but allowed Dad a chance to organize what was packed in the back of the station wagon. In phone conversations with James, a plan to purchase and deliver booze from Illinois was devised. Cases of the preferred brand and type could be picked up in Streamwood and be transported along with our luggage to South Carolina. It was a detailed effort to make the purchase and then navigate 741 miles to the rural community outside of Spartanburg, South Carolina.

In the effort to hire a cadre of workers to establish the plant, James hired Tom to lead their trucking and transportation department. He moved to the distant location, affirming a logical step for his career and keeping alignment with the circle of friends. He purchased a nearby home and remained a part of the social interaction made closer in the new location where new friends were scarce. Tom bought a husky from a local farmer and adapted to the new pattern and framework of the South.

As we arrived in the driveway, welcome hugs from Grace sparked laughter and quick responses from Dad on the long journey and our precious cargo. Dispatching with the luggage, we unloaded cases of booze into their basement storage. The arduous task was a matter of discussion in the coming days, a challenge to the county restrictions and a victory in delivering bottles of treasured brew. Canadian Mist, a staple in the creation of the Manhattan, a cocktail made with bourbon and vermouth, had arrived by the cases and would fuel conversations and laughter with old friends.

Our arrival in South Carolina created the reunion my parents sought, a chance to see old friends whose life and experience so closely mirrored theirs. On the basement level, there was a television and a new video game system that quickly caught my attention. Even though only black and white, the system replicated Pong, the tennis-like video game that I had played at the arcade for a quarter. Simply turning it on and using the controller, the game offered unending amusement with a switch. Fascinated by the innovation, the system drew my teenage focus and attention.

The first invitation was to see the dog, a sparky animal that had an allure because we knew the breed was native to far away Alaska. The unique features of the dog and the chance to see his home drew interest. And fear. And a reminder that what I packed to bring on this trip was the secret. It traveled with me even when I thought it was left behind. Seven years had passed since the first interaction with pajamas and the tickle game. The invite to play with his dog was a subtext for Tom inviting my sister and I to stay overnight at his house.

I argued that we should play Pong for a little longer, a plea for time, inviting my sister to another round of this new object of interest. She enjoyed the game with me and shared my assessment that the game system was great and an unexpected item for home entertainment. In the first days of our visit, we had burned through daily rain showers, using it as a hiding place. We made small challenges for our play and tallied the games played. Just imagine the quarters we saved.

The pattern of agreeing to suggestions by other adults drew my sister and I into the tangles of Tom's invitation. We packed a small bag with bathroom items and clothes for the next day. After dinner together, we went to the basement on the way out to grab our bag and make the trip to his home. By now the sun was setting, and I imagined that the fear I had would soon end with sleep.

Tom's Cutlas was an attractive car that fit snugly between the sports car category and a more mature vehicle. A rumbling exhaust system provided a way to notice this stylish ride, an outlet for his interest in cars and a means to engage others. He invested in the car stereo complete with cassette player and improved speakers. We couldn't just ride in the two-door car to his place. First, we needed a detailed tour of the vehicle. There were so many features. The stereo played songs we liked. The Doobie Brothers sounded better on cassette. The muffler roared even lower when you pressed on the gas. His pride for this car continued, "You should sit behind the wheel." I took inventory of the attributes of this shiny car and saw his approach anew, highlighting areas of interest and levering his perspective. He wanted us to see the car as a way to see him, something that had unique features to be appreciated. Certainly, we would think that was cool.

Debby liked the car. Most people did. Part muscle car and with all the accouterments that made the car attractive. The extra trim and the chrome air filter, each of these were selected as part of his hobby interest in cars. As the vehicle orientation continued, I began to question if she was being drawn in as well. Was the car like his invitation for me, when all this mysterious pattern began, to get pancakes?

Pulling into his driveway, I looked for the dog, hopeful for a distraction and object to occupy our time. I thought of our long trek to South Carolina smuggling booze and the adventure of delivering cases to old friends. And I realized that I had packed my heavier baggage, the secret and scabs from many years. How could it be that seven years had passed since this infection first began? Why did I fear it the same way that paralyzed me when it all began? How was the emotion so far away yesterday, but now, pulling uphill in the driveway, anxiety covered me with fear and memories of the things I hated most about my life.

The Cutlas door closed smoothly as we walked to the front door, entering into his space again after such a long time. The husky dog was there for greeting, a furry bundle of energy and a chance to do something with what I felt. I kneeled to pet her, realizing that Tom had wandered into the living room and was outlining the evening. Yes, he thought, we should take a shower before bed.

Deb dismissed the idea with a glance, but quickly stepped into the bathroom to abide by the direction. As she stepped in and closed the door, I felt it again. Alone. With him.

From the moment of the first touch, I felt differently about who I was and recognized that something was wrong. It naturally plagued me when confronted by Tom, but persisted and changed the way I felt about myself. More nervous around people. Less confidence I was doing the right thing. Cautious that others would notice I was out of step. Frequent stutters in speaking. Not sure that my dents and odd discovery was known to others. Worried that a secret would ruin me. Ashamed that the blemish ever took root, and especially disgraced that I had somehow allowed it. For years.

And with time, the magnitude of guilt grew knowing I had submitted to something I could never imagine. Or forget.

The bathroom door was closed and the chance to focus on the dog was waning. The questions began. Each was a check-in on a previous status of school, grades, and social activity. Each one was punctuated by a jestful tease and critique for how I was not hitting the mark.

Ironically, emotional pain as a boy had fueled a strong interest in shedding any label or perception that I was stained. Despite Collins' attempts to convert me to a right-handed world, I worked harder to outlast the feelings I had inside that I was not created right. In school subjects I enjoyed, I studied with more intent, finding a way to invest. Having absorbed my dad's commentary and disinterest in the French horn, I practiced in earnest, finding a space to think deeply inside the melodies and orchestration.

I carefully navigated our conversation to a topic that I believed would be unassailable: my election to the Student Senate at the end of eighth grade. As Tom's questions persisted, I guarded myself for criticism that I was not enough. To be elected required a campaign, and voting by hundreds of students after short speeches given by student candidates. The position held little prestige, but it had been an outlet for uplifting my self-worth. But he knew that would take time and that I should be studying. And would I ever have a girlfriend? Achievement squashed. Dilemmas continued.

My replies were inartful and incomplete. I felt the beam focus on his inquiry and it easily eroded what confidence I had salvaged since our last encounter. The shame I felt sparked back brighter, again adding stock to convictions I harbored from the first touch. He moved closer to me, grabbing the collar of the dog and pulling her to the garage to be let out. He returned to me asking how much I weighed now, staring at me in disapproval. His hand moved quickly to my waist, unexpectedly, and before I could reposition. My belt, he said, was too loose, and he pulled it and me from side to side.

Heat rose to my face as I turned and looked to the door where the dog stood waiting to come back inside. His hand moved the belt more with his added description of how pants should fit. The scent of an evening's cocktail flushed to my nose. The belt could be tighter, he suggested, pulling on it to move me to his front as his eyes looked into the buckle. I shook inside and wished the dog would bark. My face flushed and my stomach hurt, knotted by the returning capture of his hands.

The view of the dog became more intense as I felt dizzy. I stared at her slowly, closing my eyes and wishing I was out of my body.

The door burst open with Deb's laugh and announcement that her shower was done, a task she hated and was glad to cut short. The air stood still. Tom was startled by this action that he had not predicted.

At that moment, I drew my attention to my sister, seeing her smile still present from her bath exit and exclamation. I took in the light coming from the bathroom and then returned to see her look at me. I realized then she saved my life. She had escaped from the bath requirement, and by her expeditious timing, Tom's pursuit concluded, never to appear again. I moved quickly to the mirror, closed the door completely, and turned the water fully to hot.

It was true that Student Senate took up time and became a focal point for me trying to outshine my pimples and overcome awkwardness. Ninth grade was a more complex time, one with expectations for social structure, appearance, and the strong internal voice that doubted my status. A day in school included busy hallways to interact, avoid, or take in the ranking that naturally took place with teens. It was more difficult with low self-esteem and a persistent voice that feared discovery.

When a friend asked if I could help run the sound board for the next play, I was interested enough to attend the first meeting and auditions. Including everyone in the process, the director insisted even the technical roles supporting the play would audition. That exercise in team building netted my selection for the lead part, not my aspiration or desire.

Making matters worse, the lead male role had a romantic relationship inside the story that included a kiss. A requirement to actually kiss another person.

Memorizing lines was not the most difficult part. Taking on the attributes of a grown man and expressing words that were not mine was well beyond my comfort zone. I made cassette tapes with the lines that

I could play and repeat to absorb and memorize pages of script. I played the cassette in the evening and let it play as I went to sleep. I picked different starting places for the dialogue, accumulating understanding of the theme and slowly putting the words in the right order. Repeating them out loud in rehearsals tuned me into the tape and away from my own feelings about the words.

The movements on stage were all prescribed as part of the script, setting the requirement to move toward the female character to show the love interest. It never felt normal. Lines of script said words I would never say. The script said to look into her eyes and tell her the way she made me feel. And there was supposed to be a kiss.

The director's experience with teens in plays made him familiar with hesitancy and import of a kiss between two characters in a play. The nervousness was not invisible, and he created a separate rehearsal to work through those lines and sequences in the play. That should have made it easier.

Sharon, the actress for my clumsy love interest, was popular by any standard, and my own crush interest grew. She tolerated the long pause I created in avoiding the kiss and accepted that I hugged her instead. We never spoke about it. And then there was the special rehearsal. Directions to move this close, and then say the line looking her in the face. I got to the cheek but never cleared the obstacle of my own fear of actually kissing. It was not because I was not interested.

Lights in the auditorium dimmed and the curtain opened on our play and the event that should have culminated in a kiss. I was nervous about remembering my lines. Nervous that I would move to the right place. Nervous that Sharon would actually see into my feelings. And petrified that when the lights covered the stage, they would illuminate me and clearly show how incapable I was of completing this simple task. They might see a mistake in the recitation from the script. Or they might see me clumsily move to the wrong place. And with a spotlight, it would not be hard to see I never kissed her, paralyzed by my own deep fears and competing narrative.

Two weeks after two evening performances, she and I held hands walking through the halls of a local community center. Somehow, she had not discounted the not-as-popular boy and the guy who didn't muster the courage to actually follow through on the kiss. No number of rehearsals would have brought me through the anguish.

Listening to music together, I felt her close and smelled the face wash she used to keep her skin clear. It worked. She was warm next to me and the conversation about pop music drew us together. Even with her braces, the moist connection of her lips warmed me and captured my imagination. Not sure it was actually happening, I pulled back a bit and then leaned in again to a place of comfort. It was the magic of our kiss and not a requirement for theater.

Summer came and soon the prospect of high school drew near. She had ample momentum as a girl with a wide circle of friends, status as a cheerleader, and natural confidence. My own summer included a start at a lumber yard and a means to save for a car. Bike rides took me there, and longer hours allowed me to save for transportation and a measure of freedom. Our feelings and relationship waned, leaving me with more time to work and more questions about my candidacy as a man. Teenage romance was over, as was the two-act play and the experiment with a kiss.

The flurry of hall activity at the high school dwarfed the dimensions of ninth grade. Several schools were merged at that level, raising the stakes for the social ranking and more clearly defining the roles. Athletes were "jocks." Kids who smoked pot were "freaks." Popular people enjoyed their own fame and acceptance. I was neither. In fact, not having a girlfriend to pin my ranking cast me to the crowd of the unnoticed. If there had been a chance to crawl the ladder, an inability to perform in a play and the fleeting duration of a teenage crush caused me to miss the step. Oddly, I was not cast for the part.

CHAPTER 6

Bike Ride From Darkness

JAMES AND GRACE CAME TO the house. They were close allies and friends over many years who had moved to a nearby town two years prior to our family moving. In some way, they influenced a number of decisions, the first of which was to leave the stable but sad limits of Streamwood, Illinois. Our families had grown up in houses only blocks apart, and while the floorplan was similar, they had a pool that became a magnet for gathering. When they moved to nearby Bartlett, even though it was merely three miles away, they moved for the allure of a better life.

The new house was made of brick, a raised ranch with a completely furnished basement. This was a substantial upgrade from the 900-square-foot factory home that comprised hundreds of homes and winding streets in Streamwood, the city with a smile. In fact, there was a fireplace in the basement of their new place to create a recreation space with a pool table and casual bar. Indoor carpeting, tall trees surrounding the house, and a street mailbox were only a few of the many upgrades. We saw their new house and only thought they had truly made it across the finish line with a brick exterior and abundant space with two floors. By comparison, our 750 square feet, three-bedroom house seemed so modest, so small, and unworthy.

When we finally did move to Bartlett, we landed in a home with two floors, but in reality, one was finished and the other was a utility basement. My dad had a weekly driving route that went through Bartlett and when James and Grace moved, that drive became his journey to envision the life he really wanted to live. He made mention of breaking free from the less than average imprint in a city that had no inherent smiles. After a few walkthroughs and real estate arrangements, we rented a truck and enlisted the help of church families to pick up pieces and disassemble the bunk beds my father made that never moved. It was an evolution to a town that we perceived as having prestige. Afterall, the town had the train station and also the bank. There was even a golf course on the edge of the village, a main street, and all the suburban accouterments.

There were a number of excuses for invites and gathering of friends to our new abode. In the winter shortly after we moved in, James and Grace came to visit our place. They brought with them friends from Indiana that over the years we had met and shared camping experiences. They fit into the social exchange and had kids of their own that were in the band of ages for all the families.

When they came over it was January, a cold night that had refrozen ice melted by the sun earlier in the day. The invite was somewhat extemporaneous with no substantial reason or milestone. But it quickly became a festive evening for the adults, laughing fueled by cocktails, stories, and eventually my dad's strumming of old songs on a ukulele. It was a scene repeated from camping where there was an affinity shared by the adults. Their kids were teenagers, their life station seemed more stable, and, for us, we had finally made our way across the railroad tracks. The fellowship was increasing in volume and laughter when the invite came.

"Go to our place," was the suggestion from Grace. Others joined in the encouragement. Once it was presented, I was attune to the fact that my sister was not home that night. She had left prior to the arrival to babysit. And so the suggestion soon turned to direction so the adults would have the evening to themselves. Somehow, I should be entertained, they thought, even though I would have been just as happy to remain at home.

"Josh and Cindy are there," was the report and basis for the premise that I should leave and go to James and Grace's. Their kids were two and four years older than me and I felt no particular affinity to them absent the group of other kids that socialized together. But refuting the invitation seemed impossible and so I went to the garage, deciding to ride my bike there. It was too cold, they said, but for me it added something of a challenge that I could enjoy.

Weeks after we moved to Bartlett, I met a local boy who delivered the newspaper. He had a basket mounted to the front of his bike and it was usually packed with papers. On Saturdays he had a real challenge with thick papers with advertisements. He made two trips on the bike that day, going from his home and then returning to refill for the second load of papers. When he asked me to take the route while he was on vacation for two weeks, I thought of the cash that I could earn. According to his report, he collected almost five dollars a week. I imagined buying jeans for fourteen dollars and getting a hair styling for twelve. No more no-name pants and barbershop haircuts. The weekly earnings seemed like a rich reward for driving the bike and delivering the Elgin Courier News. So, I was quick to accept his offer to take over the route and soon bought baskets for my three-speed. He had found new interests after vacation, but that was a breakout opportunity for me.

I mastered the route of houses for delivery and the route of afternoon papers for weekdays and two morning papers on the weekend. Setting an alarm for wakeup was part of the joy as was loading the basket and shoulder bag to carry my route. Green rubber bands went around the paper, a process I learned during the vacation trial. Each paper was rolled tightly and the band wrapped two or three times to keep it firm. The resulting inked hands became a daily routine for the next three years.

The bike and papers were part of my liberation. There was a recurring task to drive either morning or evening. Duty called me away from home and made me adventure into the streets and to the people that were on my route. The economics were compelling to me, and in footsteps, I dreamt about the things that money would buy. There was even a chance to earn a tip from the $1.25 I collected from each patron, an accumulation of singles and coins that I saved in order to buy clothes that matched my peers. No more Sears Roebuck jeans or off-brand shirts. No more barbershop or haircuts from Dad. I could afford the outfits, and after all, it wasn't Streamwood anymore.

So, when I was boxed into leaving for James and Grace's, I thought of my trusted bike and their house that was only a few blocks beyond the route I had memorized. Temperature and cold were not a constraint as I had learned the path on sidewalks that was clear of snow or ice. The process of discovery included a number of falls, each of them dumping newspapers in the crash. But riding allowed efficiencies in time and reduced the need for returns to refill the carry bag. Baskets and speed on the bike were the advantages that outshined the cold, the rain, and the risks.

In one season of selling the newspaper to new customers, I earned enough points from the Courier to get a light for the front and back of the bike. The light included a spring-loaded mechanism that, when released, pushed the small wheel to the bike tire and generated power for the lights. The intensity of the light changed with increased speed but seemed so efficient; it was an object of fascination for me that inspired my door-to-door campaign to get new subscribers for the courier.

With the light on, I closed our garage and saw my breath and the light hitting the street en route to their home. I had forgotten a hat but quickly pulled my hood around my face, but not before the cold chilled me and the dry air stung my face. I navigated the known parts of the sidewalk and street that were clear. By January there had already been several snowstorms, and there was a dingy gray and white snow that persisted over every winter until March. The light from the bike was effective in showing the glare of spots where melting now had again frozen to ice.

The deep chill made me ride more quickly in an attempt to decrease my exposure with a steady wind pouring into my hood. I took some pride in navigating through the details of sidewalks, streets, and the ability to ride a bike through these winter days. As a veteran of my route, I learned to work beyond the season's expectations, and this cold night was no different. Peddling past the last block of my paper route, I saw their house in the distance and increased my tempo to get there and get warm.

I was anxious about the awkward truth of our disparate ages and lack of true connection as friends. Josh seemed more of a trouble maker, one of the many in that group that drank beer in the shadow of our parents long before it was approved. I stared at the house, again with envy for its stature and thought of the upgrades from our vinyl-sided smaller place many blocks away. There was a porch light in the back that I could see from the block before I turned. I planned my entrance and realized how much I didn't want to be there.

Josh came to the door, not losing a chance to call me an idiot for riding a bike. It was winter after all, and didn't I know it was cold enough for a snowmobile and not a bike? "Yes," I thought, of course, but I had mastered a great skill in driving and enduring cold on my bike. He walked me to the basement where he and Cindy were playing a game of pool. The TV was on and I accepted the first offer of a beer simply to establish some credibility.

The pool game led to another and then Cindy challenged me to a game. That took another beer. She was four years older and stared at me, amused by my timid approach to the drinking. I knew immediately that she would leverage her age in comments when I missed the pool shot. And I should have another beer, she said, staring again at me and seeing the plain awkwardness of my thirteen-year-old self. The game led to darts, more drinks, and it seemed to me it mirrored the exchange of our parents. We should laugh, share some stories, and drink.

It was late when the game ended. Josh had the couch, where he fell asleep watching football. When Cindy left to go upstairs, I took a pillow and laid on the floor to watch TV too. The fireplace was still crackling, sounds that punctuated the room but soon dulled me to the sounds of football on the screen. Feeling the full weight of several beers, my head became slow and lazy. My eyes grew heavy before long as I surrendered to sleep without reservation.

Warmth surrounded my fingers. I felt breath pushed through my left hand. I wondered how my hand had moved from my body, and how the warmth led to wetness. I felt her tongue licking my finger and then sucking on it slowly. Was I dreaming? The slow drunken feeling made it unclear to me, the uncertain point in sleeping when a dream is real and it's not known that we will ever wake.

Cold air covered my fingers. And then the warmth was there again when she moved my hand inside her shirt. Her hand held my finger and pressed it to her nipple. She used it as an instrument of her own, rubbing it against her breast, circling her arousal and attempting to spur mine. In the moments of awakening from this dream, I stumbled over what was real and actually happening. I clenched my eyes closed recognizing I now had to solve the puzzle of how to avoid these moves.

Before truly awakening, she moved my hand more completely and it was then I knew her shirt was open. She continued to move my hand to where she wanted, leading me to either join in her interest or move to avoid it continuing. I withdrew my hand slowly, a contrived move intended to imitate restless sleep, and turned my head so I could roll over to my stomach. The adjustment was a decision made quickly as I felt twisted by the effect of the alcohol and the surreal experience of her pursuit. Hopeful that I had faked a normal sleep maneuver, I sighed a breath. Maybe she understood the pursuit was unsuccessful. Maybe she accepted that the lure had not stirred me to romance or physical involvement. Maybe she would see that her angle did not draw me in, and maybe she would just end the touching that she wanted from me.

My hand moved again. I felt her stir next to me and soon her leg was next to mine. I struggled to imitate a person fully asleep who was pliable and not awakened by the movement near me. But her hand moved mine and soon I felt her warm skin and the zipper from her jeans that were now pulled down. She breathed into my ear as her hand pulled mine to touch her. Knowing that my acting was incomplete, I felt panic as my sleeping scene would soon be discovered. She pulled my hand to her, moving my fingers to touch her. My arm was moved and her leg was over mine with deeper breathing in an invite I could not accept.

My ears were ringing and heart racing when I knew I had to escape. This was not a dream. This was not the date with a girl that I once imagined. This was inescapable without a crisis. I considered the few options remaining to move or adjust. I thought about ways to wake up or how I could actually fake being passed out completely. I had expended the rollover option. My fake sleeping would soon be discovered. Fear overtook me.

Startled, I moved to my feet too quickly and the drunkenness made me unstable to fully stand. I looked away from Cindy and mumbled I had to leave. No words made sentences but were stuttered and incomplete. She made no response and only lain on her side like a Rubenesque portrait posed for appreciation. Her glare to me was not disappointment, but a sly smile shown to a fool. She beamed into my brokenness and exposed the part I continually tried to hide. Josh appeared passed out on the couch. My head turned from the backward glance, but I knew my shortcoming had been unveiled. The normal and expected response to advantage the proposition did not take place, and she was sure to find ways to share the fearful boy story with others. The fireplace was calm in opposition to my fight-or-flight response. I missed the first step of the stairs from the basement heading to the garage, my recovery led me up two steps in a noisy exit from this place.

I never imagined an interlude with Cindy. My boyhood crushes at school never prospered, a common plight explained by chance and the wit of an awkward boy. I did imagine that one day there would be a match for my interest, someone who stirred me with her looks and ability to laugh at my jokes. Cindy was neither, making her aggression so much more complicated and something I never anticipated.

Out of breath, the cold again swept over me with my jacket not zipped and no hood to cover my head. The light flickered as I came up to speed and turned from the driveway to the sidewalk and street. Breathing deeply, my exhale showed a fog exhaust in the moonlight and was the spark for release. Tears came to my cheeks and stung with the cold and grew as my fears overtook my breathing. I shuttered and peddled trying to steer the bike and keep in the narrow path I knew could take me home without incident.

Standing on the pedals, I worked harder to gain speed and raced to be safe again. The crying grew to sobbing as I thought of how I had been discovered as incomplete, vulnerable, and again the victim of unwanted touches. How did she know? How did she see the marker of my primary defect and advantage her own desire? And how could it be that another experience infected me with the spoils of touch? It was more evidence that I was forever damaged in this way, and that the teenage boy could not evolve to a different or even normal physical relationship. What was it, after all, that proved a marker that others saw and used as permission? And even worse, the evening netted another person who could testify as to my weakness. I imagined her own gossip to drunken Josh and that she may one day share this story of how unnatural I was and unable to accept her approaches like a real man. I ruminated on her criticism of me and thought about my incompleteness staring into the sidewalk.

Entering the street three blocks from home, I looked into the corner where the sewer was surrounded by ice and gray snow. The edge had ice and the concrete curb bulged over the years, rising above the street by two inches. I adjusted quickly to level up to the sidewalk from the street, but the front wheel came up, hitting the gap before

I could turn to avoid the jolt. I shook and the baskets and bike rattled loudly when the wheel hit the curb. The bike halted abruptly, tumbling me over the bike and into the frozen grass and ice. My jacket, still unzipped, allowed snow into my shirt. Two years of navigating these streets gave me no immunity to the collapse and ability to avoid the obstacles.

It was then that I fully released my tears, allowing the shock of my fall to cover the panic that fueled my midnight bike ride home to escape Cindy. My elbow hurt and my leg hit the basket before I landed in the grass. The streetlight shined on me, baring my error and weakness as I stared into the light, realizing that I was visible to neighbors. I heaved with sobbing and knew it was a race now to get away from this night and the feelings that overwhelmed me. The streetlamp rose above me casting light into my failure and allowing others to witness. I must get out of this place before others see inside of me and into this crying boy.

Pulling my bike forward, I moved it upright to the sidewalk where I could continue the escape to my dark room and basement in our house. And if I did it quickly, perhaps I could avoid discovery and any retelling of the events that began with a pool game and ended with my panic and stumble up the stairs. Raising my leg over the bike as I had done so many times before proved that the front tire had popped when it slammed into the curb. The wheel would not turn evenly, it wobbled and thumped where the curb dented the rim. There was no way to generate light from the lamp powered by a gear.

Grabbing the handlebars, I walked alongside the bike, attempting to recover and shake off the fall and its consequences. My footsteps crunched the snow and the front tire bumped with each rotation. My breath poured out a trail before me as the frozen air dried the tears on my face. I wiped away moisture from my running nose and saw the cars parked in our driveway. Turning into the last sidewalk before home, I planned my quick entrance into the back door. I considered how I could avoid being noticed by the parents and forced into some description of the evening.

With the bike back in the garage, I quickly zipped up the coat and headed for the steps to enter the house. Looking through the kitchen, I was fortunate to spot my mother as she was deeply engaged with Grace. I raised my hand in a quick wave and only caught a portion of her response before I quickly trailed the stairs to my room. Turning on a light and throwing the jacket on the bed, I first noticed the tear in my pants. Jeans that my paper route had earned for me were torn at the knee and likely ruined for sure.

Before closing the bedroom door, I turned for the light to the basement and saw the refrigerator to my right. I pulled it open and saw the cream sherry wine that once made me feel warm. I opened it quickly and raised it to my lips. And again. Again. The warmth brought back the swirl of intoxication and the lift from this moment. I swallowed and moved to the quick space of the bedroom hoping my head would soon escape the knowledge that it was not over. The Jordache designer jeans were ruined, my bike and escape vehicle were broken. The feelings from a young boy with loose pajamas came to me in waves. I settled into rest but was unable to get away from the angst of these touches and spillover they created.

CHAPTER 7

Allerton

IN ORDER TO LOWER THE cost of renting a tuxedo for my high school senior prom, I joined three friends in helping a local men's clothing store market rentals. Doing so meant picking three different tuxedos and wearing them to school for those days while handing out cards. The others savored this showcase opportunity and drew attention in our fancy attire and the chance to be noticed. My challenge was twofold in that I was required to wear the tux but also needed to find a date.

My longtime girlfriend dumped me before Christmas, and even by March of the new year I had not fully absorbed the change with few prospects for the dance. I had imagined wearing the tux as a way to create an opportunity. It was a little counter intuitive. Since I was wearing the tux, it may have been assumed that I was going to attend the dance, but I certainly would not attend without a date.

Walking the busy hallway dressed in a white tuxedo, I was fortunate to see Jan from a distance and seized the chance to speak with her. "Yes," I admitted, "I do feel dorky," and she smiled, agreeing that I was out of place. "Actually," I began, "I wanted to know if you would go to the prom with me?" I raced through the sentence and hoped, even in the short delivery, that she might consider me as a prospect and say she would think about it. She would not have expected the query as we were friends, perhaps distant ones, and the senior prom was a big ask. For her to consider me as a date would have been a win. Jan was too honest for that. She smiled in her reply, letting me know she had made a commitment with another friend. Seeing my disappointment, she was quick to color the letdown as a promise she made just to attend, and not because they had interest in one another. It was a disappointment.

Two other prospects were similarly obligated, or so they said, and in an instant, the pool of prom candidates drew too small for me. Tuxedos can perhaps do many things, but they are not persuasive. I had chosen friends that had potential, but my clumsy invite sounded desperate. Dressing in a tux did not help that. I felt foolish about having walked the halls all dressed up for a dance I would not attend. But, on the other hand, no one would likely make that correlation until the day of the dance. I would not be there.

In the waning season of high school leading to graduation, I was invited with three other students to a weekend music retreat. Competition and auditions for Allerton were completed in the winter but decisions were made with hundreds of applicants. Our band teacher spent months helping us prepare before we sat in a room and recorded our audition tape. The invitation was prestigious and offered a weekend to rehearse and perform with small ensembles in brass and strings with students from across the state. The venue was a mansion from the late 1800s, converted to use by the University of Illinois, that brought the best student musicians together with conductors from the leading programs in the state.

Tall ceilings and long staircases punctuated the front entrance, an intimidating and noble building where we would live and learn for the next three days. Walking to the lobby, I wondered if the worn jeans and wrinkled shirts I packed were up to standard. Preppy shirts and Top-Sider shoes were the obvious choice for most, a wardrobe miss on my part. My appearance wasn't the only aspect of my attending that was out of step.

My quintet included two trumpet players, a trombone, tuba, and French horn. As I greeted each of them, I soon realized they had quite a portfolio of experience. Each played in a community orchestra outside their high school band. The trombone player was in a jazz ensemble that played weekend gigs. The lead trumpet actually played with the Chicago Lyric Opera, a semi-professional role that caused him to join the union so he could be paid. The other played in the Chicago Junior Symphony. I was merely the best horn player in my high school, and the limits of that notoriety were evident with each note. Each of us by now had mastered the audition piece, one that would be played in our Sunday recital. That effort got us here. But now what could we play together?

The weekend at Allerton was dedicated to elevating our ability in small ensembles, and the prospect included music that was more complex. In rehearsals, I learned about each of the players in my group, a steady and accomplished set of musicians. Each spoke with clarity about their next steps to college and the ways they would leverage their musical ability. One intended to teach, but each had a clear view of what would happen in a matter of weeks after we departed from the Victorian grounds of Allerton.

With excellent players by my side, the audition piece quickly rose in caliber and the rehearsals for that music required little additional work. A baroque piece had been arranged for a brass ensemble and we practiced it at a slow tempo, recognizing its complexity and sus-tained movement. A fugue uses a musical theme that can be traded and repeated between instruments to create an engaging experience for the listener. What one instrument plays in one part is repeated by another, perhaps in a different volume or with an added context. In order to work, each of the ensemble members are required to keep tempo and blend from one part to the other consistent with the shared theme of the movement.

We decomposed the baroque piece necessarily in order to find parts we could learn to play slowly. Once mastered, we picked up the tempo, aiming at 120 beats per minute that was the composer's intent. The baroque style had few long notes and instead challenged the listener by continual movement of the main melody and the alternate, to draw even more interest, passing it like a baton from one instrument to the other. Keeping pace with what seemed like a track race to me was extremely frustrating. Our band teacher had been relentless in his preparation, and without it, I was dithering through the pages, rarely keeping pace. The first day had quickly expended the learned equity I had in the audition piece, and the baroque music was a new challenge.

Disappointed by my inability to keep up with the group, our group advisor suggested he and I meet separately to rehearse. He was a college professor, an accomplished horn player, and a quiet influence. Intimidated by the prospect, I agreed but interpreted his invitation as remedial work for the less talented player. As we sat next to one another, he played alongside me with his own horn, giving me the fresh chance to hear the correct way to play each passage. This demonstration helped immensely, although it was still a difficult task to keep pace because missing a few notes took me completely off track. The advisor, now seeing my dilemma firsthand, commented, "you can't sight read, can you?" I stumbled to respond that I could, but my words faded off without completing the sentence. He struck a chord suggesting that my flaw was that I could not digest the material like the others. It was undeniable. He went back to demonstrating the next passage. And the next.

By the next day, I was in a better place with baroque, albeit with cautions that if I missed even the most minute detail, I was out of the running. The fugue was like a train that was boarded as it was already in motion, causing one to focus on the open door and the appropriate time to step up. We took our rehearsal technique further. Now at 90 beats per minute. Let's do 100. My errors were baked into each evolution, and it frustrated me to see so clearly how my deficits were impacting the group. They were each so talented. The arrangement so neatly traded melody and theme. On some iterations I survived longer than others, but my ability to play it without errors was dwarfed by the other more serious members of the ensemble.

In a break when the advisor was away, I took the opportunity to apologize. It was clumsy like wearing a tux without a date, but I was a French horn player without a baroque movement. The others were kind in receiving my regrets and agreeing that sight reading was not my strong suit, if I had a suit. Each seemed to quietly accept that there would be limitations to our recital effort, just two pieces, one that was excellent and the other that was a roll of the dice.

The aspiring teacher, a trumpet player whose identity was tied to his instrument, turned behind him and took a small bag from his case. We watched his movement closely and wondered what he was getting out. He smiled shyly as he pulled out sheet music and began to tell us about attending "Composer Camp" at the University of Illinois. We were impressed at the sophistication of his attendance and imagined how bright he must be beyond the limits of his own horn. He could interpret music from more instruments, with different keys and with an ability to make them create songs and melodies of interest. Impressed with his remark, we turned to each other again questioning his motive in sharing.

"This," he began with pages of music in hand, "is actually my favorite piece of music that I have ever heard in any version." The others joined my curiosity, looking more intently as he explained, while still questioning the relevance. "The melody to the Largo belongs to the English horn, you know, the woodwind like the oboe, that is so rare." We were still not making the connection. "So here, in these pages," he drifted off, putting his head down and forming a small smile. "Here is my version, except that I took this lyrical masterpiece and transposed it for the brass quintet." He waved the sheet music side to side to further make his case. His head returned to level, and his smile brightened. I now better understood his accomplishment but fell short of knowing what made him smile.

"What if?" he suggested, recognizing he had attracted our intrigue, as he slowly described a plan for our group to practice his new rendition of Dvorzak's "Largo." The music was from the 9th Symphony, the second movement of four, dubbed the New World Symphony. We could take on this piece as a substitute. Except that they expected the baroque piece. Programs were printed and named the fugue and composer with precision. We chatted about this modest act of disobedience. Smiles erupted with the others and through his descriptions and details, learned that his version held longer phrases, emotional interludes with a powerful refrain versus the churning repetition of the planned piece. He seized the moment, reaching for his trumpet to play the first phrase, a strong and powerful theme that captured the room and evidenced its merit. The notes rang through the tall ceilings, and his subtle tremolo created waves of sound that increased with his crescendo. It was not just the melody, this passage evoked a message, the bright prospect of the New World now delivered in this brass highlight. He lowered the trumpet from his mouth and leaned forward to pause for our reactions. He knew he had us. We smiled then, agreeing without words to this alternate plan and accepting the risk that it may not be well received. We were assigned one piece. We would be playing something else completely off script.

Over the chatter of dozens of students and players at dinner, our rogue trumpet player detailed Dvorak and this particular movement. An immigrant to the United States in the 1700s, the composer wrote the 9th Symphony as a way to express his gratitude for this great experiment, a new land far from the torn Europe he left behind. Dvorak came to the New York Conservatory at the invitation of an heiress who wanted to produce European symphonic music in the States. As he detailed this character from Czechoslovakia, he drew us into the history of this special piece, adding meaning to our unexpected rendition.

His lesson continued.

After creating the 9th Symphony, a student of Dvorak named William Arms Fisher built upon the work adding lyrics reflective of the spirituals that would have been sung in fields and at work in early America. Originally named the New World Symphony, with Fisher's lyrics, the Largo Movement was many times now referred to as "Goin' Home." This title and aspect added important content to the movement, giving voice to the growing tension in the melody that is triumphantly resolved in its end. Indeed, as the title inferred, the listener hears the music telling the audience they are headed to rest, they are "goin' home."

His voice continued a bit louder and without interruption from the activity or voices around us, as he recited the lyrics to us, thereby proving the merit of this piece and giving us reasons to accept its important message. We were all mesmerized by his oration:

> It's not far, just close by,
> Through an open door;
> Work all done, care laid by,
> Goin' to fear no more.

Tuning into his delivery, I became lost in the lyrics and laid claim to the last line. If we are to play for the recital, and if we step off script to play something that is equally complex and yet far more meaningful, we should fear no more. I felt that sense of empowerment extend beyond the limits of Allerton and wondered if it translated to my apprehension for the recital the next day, the prom dance I would not attend, and ultimately the path I was roaming toward that seemed different than others.

As scheduled, our recital was Sunday afternoon in a large dining room of the mansion reconfigured with chairs for performers and seating for a large audience. Looking around the room, I again noticed my downgraded clothes and the gravitas of this venue. It was a serious place whose tall ceilings offered rich music to reflect from one wall to another, creating a modest reverb and subtle sophistication. The instruments rang from the walls. Groups assembled from across the state performed their pieces and were received with applause before they briefly bowed and waited for the next group to quickly occupy the chairs. In the front, in position to be the next ensemble, I looked over the audience and considered their collective expertise, each with bona fides as great musicians with an interest in hearing the level of performance that took place at Allerton.

As predicted, our first piece rang true to our mastery of the written work and included our own interpretation of the dynamics. The atmosphere complimented this well-played music. I looked at our advisor in the third row just before switching the music on the stand to "Goin' Home." I wondered how upset he would be at our choice and disobedience. Without his knowledge, we were swapping out the right number from the program and adding our own contribution. I was convinced, and especially by the passion of our Dvorak aficionado trumpeter, that this powerful song would resonate. The long and leading first strains were led by trumpet harmony and the brass ensemble was layered to the background. As the song moved to the center, the melody drawing to a point of conflict, the arrangement gave the lead to the French horn. The musical phrase tested the upper range of the horn, but I filled it with air, leaning into this moment and what our song conveyed. In reaching for the high note, I closed my eyes to savor it, hearing the other brass members harmonize and support the pinnacle.

The advisor's stillness as we finished was in view. Applause from others seemed to overtake what I saw when my eyes opened again. The audience liked the version created by our trumpet player as an antidote to my imperfections with the baroque movement. By their clapping, I could imagine they understood the full context and were moved. No confusion over the written program that said it should be baroque. I was relieved and grateful, spared from the errors that were sure to appear in the scripted piece and gratified that kids I just met were so willing to take a chance.

One of our family camping friends was a professional drummer who worked in sales for the instrument manufacturer. In his role, he traveled to conventions and met with musicians to demonstrate and sell drum kits. Given his ability, he enjoyed the campfire music, often commenting that one time he would share a drum solo, perhaps on logs. He was keen to share his insights on music with me and frequently encouraged my horn playing.

Heading into high school, he was aware of a military interest and he created contacts with the military services through events he attended. He met the conductors of many of the service bands. He called me by phone to update me on his latest contact, insisting I write down the number he provided. Without saying so directly, he indicated that, after a phone call, I could audition with the service conductor. This was not the ordinary way of joining the military band, but he leveraged his contact and made that request as he scribbled their phone number in exchange for preferred treatment from his company.

The guaranteed audition never truly appealed to me, perhaps because of my apprehension of doing that job in uniform and equally because I had a realistic appraisal of my talents. I was good and not great. Getting the audition was no automatic switch for happiness and wearing a tux to school offered little promise for Prom unless the date agreed to attend.

Weeks from Allerton, I understood these conflicting realities and different options. I was not the expert musician, nor was I the naturally popular senior in high school wearing the right outfit and headed to college as expected with the others.

CHAPTER 8

Calling Home

A SMALL CLOSET HELD THE two pay phones used for calls, some made by inserting coins and other long-distance calls made with a number sequence and card. I had memorized the card some time ago and used it to make calls home to check in at admittedly uneven intervals. Having news that Dad was hospitalized made the intent to call more clear and drew me to listen even more closely.

He was surprised by his arrival at the hospital some days prior, having suffered a series of heart attacks that he never felt. But more than the absence of pain, he was dull to his own history with smoking, a decades-long habit since he was 14 and worked part time at a liquor store. Doctors performed an elaborate surgery for the era, a complicated bypass surgery at age 52 that could give him a way forward and a new lease for living.

He was more relaxed in this posture, now confined to a hospital room post surgery and struggling to grapple with the gravity of his case and its implications. Quitting smoking was akin to losing his first girlfriend, an analogy he shared in the phone call. We ran through the checklist of activities that had taken place. There was a plan for recovery, for physical therapy, and a grateful sense of humble appreciation for a new phase that would include a fully functioning heart.

In my portion of the update, I paused to share my equal disappointment that I was not going to West Point after all, but had also been accepted to the Virginia Military Institute. He asked questions I had never considered myself. Why was I headed in that direction? And what did I know about this small school in Virginia? I missed the opportunity to fully share my aspiration and blooming desire to elevate my position through education and an Army commission. He laughed when I told him I had never been to VMI but that I knew someone who went. That testimonial was missed by Dad and made me question my own path.

"You're spinning your wheels," was his reply, a critique of my tentative decision and process of applying without any firsthand knowledge of the place. In reflection, he lamented his own two years of mandatory military service with pride, repeating that he had been promoted to corporal before he finished his obligation. He could have retired at 42, would have had a stable vocation, and still considered himself young. And then, with a more angular tone, he reviewed my situation, a sergeant with under three years of service. It wasn't envy that made him criticize; it was his own contemplation of how he might have finished had he stayed in the military. I was foolish, in his estimation, for not being grateful for the early promotion and opportunity to continue to serve until retirement.

The military created a complete assortment of father figures for me. Some were harsh and few were compassionate, but they set examples I learned from. Ironically, the military became a common thread for Dad and I, something we could share without ever really sharing or fully understanding the details. His was a mandatory tour that he resisted, leaving behind the love of his life, that was an experience he treasured later in life. Mine was a voluntary tour, a decision made to leave behind the identity I liked least, hoping I could find a new way forward.

Being away from home forced a letter exchange that became the premise for our dialogue and a great insight to the man. I routinely failed at replies and made excuses for why I did not write. Uneven and inconsistent, this was a communication channel opened and one I did not experience as a child when he was immersed in a project, television, and drinking, so there was no conversation after 8:30 p.m. I had created my own distractions as well, a part-time job at a lumber yard and my own circle of friends that drew me away.

Even though lop-sided toward Dad, he shared his notes, quips, and punny humor in letters to me. In a post-typewriter era, Dad bought a thermal ink typewriter that operated on batteries and special heat-sensitive paper. His typing style must have been quicker than his penned letters, a picture of perfect lettering as a result of his military duties as a draftsman.

My attraction to the military began with identity and purpose but was also oriented in paying for college. At seventeen, the agreement of my enlistment came from my parents' signatures. Although Mom cried in doing so, she agreed with the decision and only feared her youngest would go away, drift from her and our home. She was right to hold such fears as I had them myself. But signing was a bragging point for Dad, a legacy he imagined that I followed his pathway. During Saturday chores, I witnessed the way he walked and he called a slow cadence, a singing melody to encourage me to be in step. The choice to join had many facets, but the ticket from nowhere to somewhere was its main attraction.

Like Dad had been, I was stationed at Fort Bragg in North Carolina. Once on post, the new recruits received a bus tour showing the different places, units, and barracks. It was clear to me that the 82nd Airborne Division had the best quarters. When the bus ride ended, the sergeant held a volunteer list for airborne school that would make us paratroopers who could be assigned to the 82nd. And for icing on the cake, once you completed five qualifying parachute jumps, you received an additional eighty-five dollars per month. The additional cash locked the deal for me and more than half of the bus.

Trained as a helicopter mechanic and crew chief, being at Fort

Bragg became an exciting place for a young soldier. We were the first to receive the UH-60A Black Hawk helicopter, the Army's newest utility aircraft that we flew from the factory back to the airfield. And at 18, wearing a flight suit felt like the next best thing to prestige. By saving two hundred dollars a month, I was contributing to the college fund and GI Bill, aiming for college when my term was done. Doing so still left money for beer drinking and the foolishness embedded in men. Weekend trips to the downtown bars were within budget, and when dollars were not there, pawn shops traded cash for the stereo I thought I bought to keep.

Fayetteville was a military town fitting all the stereotypes and folklore that was attractive to new recruits. Bars with dancers were great hangouts, save for the truth that it was a bar full of men glaring at topless women hoping to meet the love of their life. The daunting odds for a relationship never outweighed the interest in seeing them and fantasizing that somehow romance would spark from this dark place. A small cadre of us visited routinely, navigating the street full of hawkers telling us to go inside their place or others selling drugs.

We distinguished ourselves from other slobs, so we thought, by visiting the same place and striking a friendship with one of the dancers. When she came by our table, we bought her drinks, a house gimmick to make money, that seemed like an easy way to have a conversation. I became a regular and dismissed the expense of her ten-dollar drinks, wanting the chance to appear like we knew one another in real life. The drink was Kool-Aid, but in my mind, the dialogue was real. Maybe we actually liked one another. Maybe she thought I was cute. Maybe she thought I was a man and not a boy trying to act like a man. Maybe she did not see my fear that she would discover my secret. Maybe one day she would find out the hurt in a gentle conversation and then treasure me even more, wanting to help me overcome the memory. Maybe I was just another drunk private roaming the streets of Fayetteville, navigating the winding path in growing up.

Jumping from airplanes always captured my deepest fear in heights and especially in darkness. The repeated drill in jump school was to exit the aircraft with full equipment, lifting up six and out six inches. When the instructor yelled, "Go!" we performed our airplane exit by lifting up and pulling our arms to hold the reserve in front and bending slightly at the waist to prepare for our parachute landing fall. Prior to every jump, the unit went through a four-hour refresher sequence emphasizing all the key points prior to strapping on a parachute and waiting to load. Special roles were created for the jumpmaster, the person most trained on airborne operations and parachute rigging. No matter the rank, when performing the training or giving directions on the aircraft, the jumpmaster had both the authority and responsibility for our safety and mission.

Jumps were at night, simulating a way that paratroopers most likely would be employed in a real situation. Jump refresher began in the afternoon; there was a break for dinner and then a road march to the airfield or ride by trucks. The darkness required more direction from leaders and attention to detail at every level. In the plane, standing ready to exit, we hooked our parachute lines to an overhead cable, listening to the commands of the jumpmaster. Prior to jumping, each troop "sounded off," indicating they were hooked up, and then slapping the guy in front of them in the butt. "Ok!" was the yell that cascaded forward from both sides of the aircraft that held sixty-four jumpers, each affirming they were ready. The jumpmaster then turned his attention to the door, and after a safety check, focused intently on the light. In flight, the light was red and could be seen to the back of the aircraft. When the pilot knew they were at the right place over the drop zone, the light turned green and the jumpmaster began screaming, "Go!" This was repeated for each jumper now shadowed in green light, with jumpers pushing from the rear to hit the exit before the light went red again.

After the pure insanity of jumping into darkness, the abyss of the night absorbed our fall with the fury of airflow roaring above as the plane slowed to 150 knots per hour. The blast of air pulled and could spin the jumper upon exit. We were taught the correct tight body position to hold the spinning and air would not twist our parachute rigging. Moving your legs like you were running fast created the gyroscopic effect needed to unwind any twists created by a weak exit. The helmet strap, the ruck sack tied to our front, the emergency chute, and the rifle carrier, carried on the right side, made each jumper a heavy wind chime with little expectation that jumping into the night at 800 feet would not cause mayhem. Oddly, the rightful path of each jumper almost spun them upside down, giving each a view of the bottom of the plane as it continued forward.

An eerie but tranquil silence came over the dark landscape seconds after getting sucked through the airstream and allowing the parachute to fully open. It was not an abrupt stop, but when fully deployed, there was a perception of being suspended as a pendulum wavering from side to side. The heavy ruck sack had a single-point release cord that freed it from my waist and allowed it to fall fifteen feet, suspended underneath the jumper. The counterweight pulled the jumper from the side below as the wind made the lighter piece move. Air moving across the face was the method to consider where and how to land. The intent was to steer by pulling on the straps, hoping to land facing to the wind. This would allow the proper parachute landing fall, hitting the balls of the feet, calf, thigh, butt, and pull-up muscle. These five parts were the right sequence but frequently were missed when not facing the wind. In the dark, it was difficult to sense when a jumper would land, falling at 17 miles per hour, the equivalent of jumping from a six-foot ladder. Knowing what was on the ground was nearly impossible with only ground illumination provided by the moon and a trust that planners had lined the airplane up so jumpers could hit grass or sand.

Scanning the horizon, I saw the tree line in the distance and inhaled deeply to anticipate hitting the ground. I clicked my boots together and pressed my toes tightly to absorb the impact. Below me I saw the fading trail of a white smoke grenade set by the pathfinder, giving jumpers another way to sense the direction of the wind. I grabbed the risers on my right, again pulling and turning to align with the white smoke. The wind blew to my face causing me to squint and focus. I searched the horizon again and began to exhale, attempting to relax before the surprise landing on the ground.

I heard the scratches of branches on the ruck and then felt my body pull to the side with the line below me now lodged in the top of a tree. My remaining air escaped me and fear increased, as did my descent. The parachute quickly lost air, and with my tight body position, my arms lifted at the side of my head to protect my face. The top branches of the pine moved, snapped, and then quickly recoiled as my weight fell into the tree. Hitting the sides of my body on branches, I came to a stop as the air was pushed from my mouth with each layer of branches I fell into. My head was covered with the Kevlar helmet and easily bounced against the tree, and my face hit it straight on, injuring my nose and mouth.

I felt heat from the scratches to my face and blood now oozing from my nose. My mouth bled because my lip was cut, but deeper cuts were inside the cheek where a porcelain cap on my front teeth was now shattered. The chips and shards from the broken front tooth were easy to spit out, and the pain in my nostrils seemed to grow as I understood my condition. Holding tightly to the branch, I reached for the release cord on the ruck sack and heard it quickly fall to the ground, crashing through branches on the way down. Hugging the center of the tree, I slowly released the parachute straps on both sides and saw that I was now just a soldier almost twenty feet up in a tree. The background sounds of trucks on the ground and airplanes in the sky grew dim as I made my way down.

Five days later, my unit's first sergeant called my name to be on the next jump. I acted surprised lining up with the platoon identified to conduct refresher training. He eye-balled me and reached his big arm around me. "Confidence, kid," his solution for any fear that may have developed with my mishap. With temporary teeth and a fresh

Band-Aid on my nose, I lined up even more fearful of the outcome and with no recourse but to complete the drill. Fear had always been a part of jumping, an admission I made to the priest at the post chapel shortly after getting my wings. "A rosary," he said, "is a great protection for any danger," and should be completed in the named sequence and number he prescribed. The small beads were to be carried, and the task of completing the prayers moved your fingers from one small bead from five and then a larger bead for the recurring longer prayer. I had learned this sequence and stowed the beads in a pocket within reach while jumping.

In reviewing my fear and misfortune with jumping, I reviewed how my beads had not been fully completed. Perhaps that was why they were ineffective, or maybe this religious practice was not connected to the reality of the red light turning to green and the natural fear I had of jumping into the dark night sky. After the tree landing, I grew more critical of the beads and faced instead my disdain for the experience. I could pray that I would learn to accept the natural fear of the experience, or I pray that I would endure it. After the tree landing, I learned to pray I didn't get hurt.

On payday, I found my way to the pawn shop where a mid-week evening visit to my bar friend necessitated my use of the pawn shop to get sixty dollars. They accepted it, as they had many times before, and then I could return later to repay the loan with fees and interest. It was almost one hundred dollars to get back my stereo, a number that finally stung and made me question the process. As difficult as it was to part with the cash, I felt even more bothered by what it meant, that I was in this routine of loaning so I could drink with friends. Were they friends? It didn't take a mathematician to understand how expensive this habit had become, something that forced me to reconsider. Was I just another guy falling prey to this nightly social scene? I knew I wanted more and saw how unattractive the behavior was from my potential.

On my way to the recruiting station on the day I entered the Army, the sergeant told me to stay on track. "There are a million things that can take away your dream," he offered. As I thought of the walk past the tattoo place, street hawkers, and dark alley, I remembered his guidance. I was joining the Army to get somewhere, to move out of the below-average life I was leading. Considering my time at the airfield and exposure to the military, I saw the role of the officers who led people and worked to resource operations. I thought if I could make that rank one day, I would finally break free of my reputation and lift myself from my lower social position.

For good reason, Dad had little appreciation for officers. He didn't share my need to reinvent my identity or obviate shortcomings. His respect for that process was small, and his words reminded me of other instances where I made decisions absent his approval. "Who in the world plays French horn?" he said when I confessed my interest in the fifth grade. These comments sewed my need to learn to play, with foreknowledge that it could never be for his appreciation. Yes, the French horn was dumb, a secondary instrument, albeit with a depth in tone and range that was used in compositions to draw interest. The horn became a hiding place for me, an odd and uncommon voice in an orchestra or band. Disapproval drew me to own its uniqueness and to savor its sometimes dark and always deep intonation. His argument was then extended to my mother, "Can you name me a song that you can sing with the French horn?" She remained silent, of course. He answered his question quickly. The trumpet, he knew, was a much better instrument, evidenced by "When the Saints Go Marching In."

I learned that confining myself to his replies was a fool's errand. I accepted that my answer was wrong (to him) and knew that my own answer was a better hiding place. The affirmation would have been icing, but the cake was mine to create and accept. In the years to come, the horn became one outlet for imagining the feelings that I held inside. In Pavane, I tuned into steps not taken and love lost; in Adagio, I found solace and understanding. Learning the notes, I saw safe harbor in the instrument fitting into a larger context, a sometimes-subtle voice that complimented the overall theme.

Two short months after my call with Dad, I was discharged from the Army and made my way to Chicago for a visit with family and break before matriculating to VMI. Having celebrated my eighteenth birthday in basic training, I was short of twenty-one years old and had completed my first Army enlistment. I wore my dress green uniform on purpose, wanting that last moment to be seen that way. My flight from New Jersey included a vibrant stewardess whose attention was drawn to my attire. She shared her support and displayed a number of badges and decorations that had been given from other service members. She challenged my contribution to her apron. Enamored by her flirting approach, I pulled the last button on the green jacket and ripped it free as her concession from me. She smiled, added it to her collection, and gave me an excuse to cover the gap in a photo with Dad when I arrived home.

Dad and I, July 1984. The button is gone, a gift for the stewardess whose interest I wanted but did not secure.

Using my return as an excuse, a gathering of friends was planned on a warm July afternoon. It was the first social engagement three months after Dad's surgery and hospital stay. There was welcoming and an additional opportunity for me to articulate my reason for going to this small school in the Shenandoah Valley. I drew from my remembrance of the black-and-white printed college catalog, the only other information I had, and offered snippets to explain my direction. The truth of my direction was oriented more on the commission and re-entering the Army versus my own desire for small schools, a military setting, or a legacy dating back to 1839. Instead, I focused on the uniform, a custom-fitted assortment of grey wool and shiny buttons that would eventually lead me back to a platoon and a chance to lead. After all, I had determined, enlisted life was great work, but the officers received recognition and stature. Had I been truthful to those that asked me in July, I would have said I really wanted to leave this suburban place and reinvent myself in another life. If that meant I had to shave my head again, it was merely part of the exchange to erase my shortcomings.

The heat of summer made drinking more necessary, an environment that landed Dad in a compromised condition before dinner was served. Mom helped him to the bedroom where he agreed to pause for rest. He had recovered from surgery only weeks ago, and being twenty pounds lighter made the beer metabolize faster. He had been successful in his escape from the cigarettes, but the remaining stronghold was drinking.

Mom found me in the backyard and her concerned face helped me act quickly when she said Dad needed help in the bedroom. He was sitting on the bed when I dashed in. His head hung and he tilted slightly to the side. When I sat at his side, his tears were visible when he admitted, "I'm drunk." His assessment was accurate, judging by his slurring and the sweat beading on his forehead. He moved quickly to the bathroom and kneeled before vomiting. He groaned and labored over the bowl. He paused to remove his dentures and then leaned in again. Taking the teeth from his hand, I placed them in the sink, running cold water on a rag.

With his arms leaned into the toilet, he sobbed, feeling failure for not pacing his drinking for the event. It was a failure and an embarrassment that he thought others would notice and remember. With my hand on his side, I tried to support him, but his sobbing continued, merged with his disappointment and muttering criticisms. Indeed, he was wasted, but his slurring words were more critical of his inability and loss of stature. The cold cloth soaked the sweat from his brow and brushed saliva from his mouth.

Returning to the bed, he became more sullen, admitting he was done and not able to return to the party. Without his teeth, his cheeks were fallen and words pushed slowly to his lips. His disappointment drew him again to tears, but he was more tired now and moved to pull back the sheets to his side of the bed. I tried to offer consolation that no one would notice and that he could rest. His defeat drew his eyes from me and he leaned back to reach the pillow. Moving to the door, I saw my father resting, wondering how it was that we had just traded places in a relationship.

Two weeks later, he drove me to the airport to fly to Virginia carrying a small suitcase and an electric typewriter I bought at Sears. I was reminded of the trip I had with Dad to an in-state college before I enlisted in the Army. My prospects for affording the traditional experience were bleak, and he was clear the family did not have funds to pay tuition. And so here we were, three years later, having paid for my typewriter and still no clear vision of how my plan all fit together. I should study hard, he said, along with a bragging confidence he had that being a paratrooper with actual Army experience would earn merit at a military school. He was so right about the directions to Chicago O'Hare International Airport and so woefully inaccurate about how I would be welcomed at VMI. And so was I.

After a morning formation in September, I navigated my way to a small hallway where pay phones allowed me to call home. Mom answered hesitantly, wondering if the collect call (operator-assisted call to defer call charges to the recipient) was to give her bad news. Hearing her familiar voice calmed my breath and released a wave of sadness. Over the next several minutes, I tried to explain where I was, the absence of any welcome, and the unique adversarial system. "No," I insisted, they did not care that I had been a sergeant, and in fact, I had worked actively to keep any of those details from the other cadets in charge of my training. In being forced to follow, I surrendered, knowing it would return tenfold in leadership.

The Army GI Bill that I earned in three years would only pay for one year of college for an out-of-state student. I was offered modest offsets for tuition and took personal loans (federal loans were not in place at the time) for the remainder. The piecemeal approach to financing college made me grateful for need-based scholarships and alumni support. My mediocre grades earned me no additional support and, more often, made me question the direction I was headed.

On a cold afternoon in the fall, I exited the barracks of VMI and randomly met an alumnus who stopped me to ask questions. His first inquiry was to ask for the dinner menu that we were required to recite and memorize for each day. Thinking that he would be amused, I replied "baked ziti, salad, assorted vegetables, and cookies for dessert, Sir!" Asking me to relax, he transitioned to a gentler set of questions, asking where I was from and why I chose to attend VMI. Puzzled, I offered my incomplete assessment of why I chose this place and that I grew up in the Midwest. I was honest in sharing that it was not a place to be enjoyed and that my grades were only part of my doubt about ever making it to be commissioned. This stirred his further interest and conversation that he concluded with advice. "Show up every day and just do your part." The rest, he said, would come together with grades that might improve and support that would pay for tuition, a statement of faith with two tenets I did not fully understand.

VMI proved to be a series of obstacles and milestones that routinely challenged my goals and direction. It was easy for me to see the pathway back to an Army uniform and far more complex to accept classroom requirements as bricks for that foundation. In the undecorated and sparse conditions of the barracks, the immersion into personal and leader attributes was extended. Likely solely based on my age and not wisdom among classmates, I was elected to serve as president of the class, an enduring role that had dimensions not resident in cadet rank and assigned positions of authority. There were no stripes and term limit; the ability to gain consensus and lead peers was a mortar and pestle for developing leadership of unimagined import.

In the fall of my junior year, we were able to receive our class rings, a significant marker of the experience with a recognized token to wear. Slightly beyond the midpoint to graduation, I had met my soulmate and confidant in a summer job. She was my lovely date dressed in full-length and elegant white, as were all the guests to the dance, a reminder of the style of southern traditions: each lady wore white gloves, white dress, and carried a dozen roses. My duty to report to the school superintendent, a retired four-star general, began with a firm salute and cautious voice that our class was formed, present for our recognition to officially commence the military ball. Each date then took the gold ring from their hand to give to their cadet date. After mine was dropped, I quickly rescued it from the ballroom floor. We laughed in a portrait I could never imagine, the girl with green eyes standing near me, as she would for life, and the appearance that time might pause to allow this evolution and its satisfaction to endure.

Drifting between the noises of air rushing through the plane vents, I closed my eyes to think about the years since I started my quest. I savored the conversation I had with Dad the night before. A perpetual planner, we had discussed my arrival at Chicago O'Hare and the flight times for pick-up. This too had become our time together, as he met me at the airport over the course of three years in return trips from my enlistment. And there was always a phone call the night before the flight for specifics. So, calling the night before this flight had really been no different except for a secret that we shared and an "I love you" exchange that was not common between us.

The secret stemmed from my own evolution and the milestone of receiving the ring from VMI. Years before, I had traveled home to give my parachutist badge to Mom at a morning coffee table. After my fifth jump, the instructor gave each soldier in the platoon their own silver wings. Earning these meant agreeing to the method for presentation, the instructor took the clips off the back and punched the wings above our uniform name tapes. Mom did not really understand the importance of my gesture at the moment, but she treasured the gift and appreciated my trip home even more to complete the task. And so, Dad and I contrived a similar exchange for the class ring. A smaller version of my ring would be hers to wear, a marker of my experience and the love I had for her support.

As I wavered between needed sleep and a flurry of ideas concerning the flight home, I felt the dull bulge of that small ring box in my pocket. "Yes, it is still there," I thought. Dad and I had not discussed presenting it to Mom, but imagining he would greet me at the airport, I wanted to show him first. Inside my pocket was this small token, and in my own need for a metaphor, this was a sign of my own path forward. With this ring I was not poor, I was on an officer track, was connected to a college, and had earned something. She might be more proud now and could see this marker with the fingers that still cared for me.

Gathering my carry-on bag, I walked through the breezeway exiting from the airplane. I took a deep breath and felt the anticipation of that awaiting hug. Looking into the waiting area, I took inventory that my brother and two sisters, with their spouses, were there to greet me. Mom was adjacent to their huddle, staring straight ahead. I panned the view of my family and felt my excitement unevenly matched with their faces. I reached for Mom, to hold her and feel the reach of her arms. My head moved over her shoulder and my eyes saw a tall man with black pants standing next to her. And so, I asked the logical question,

"Where is Dad?" She pulled away from me and looked straight into my eyes, having heard my query and knowing she had a duty to reply.

She pushed me away, holding both of my hands, and mustered the sentence, "He is dead; he died this morning." My stomach knotted and I leaned into her again, searching for the complete embrace and an answer to what she had said. I buckled from the crying that overtook me, moaning and feeling the waves of tears shake me into her arms. My thoughts spun and I considered this dark surprise and how confounded it was to hear. "Where the hell is he?" I repeated and sobbed with her, shaking with each wave of tears, standing still in a crowded airport of people who continued to move around us.

I could never tire of crying or feeling angry that Dad was not there to meet me. I lifted my head from Mom's shoulder to see my sibling's faces looking down, pained again by knowing the news of his death had pierced me just as it had them hours before. I mumbled as I moved from Mom to the others to hold them, to cry again, and to feel its sting. The man in black pants moved closer, a priest from the airport staff that joined them by request to share the news. We moved to a small room nearby, and the scene drawing attention from passers-by was out of sight. We should pray, he suggested. "We should listen to his prayer?" I frowned, considering the value. Perhaps, I thought, we should just be sad that Dad is dead, and he is never coming back. And I never said goodbye. And he never saw the chapter ending. And he will miss seeing that I had changed. I would graduate from college. I would commission into the Army. I would not be the mediocre kid from Streamwood. I didn't wear pajamas anymore. I wore a uniform and had earned respect. And Mom had a ring that we thought about. But he was really gone. A chance for recognition was stolen from me.

Walking from the back of the funeral home, I stood in front of his casket dressed in the white VMI uniform I hoped to show Dad at Christmas Midnight Mass. Looking at him lying plastic in the casket, I saw his face blotched with skin-colored paints, his hands folded across his chest. Looking down, I took in the reality of his passing and imagined all of the story he would not see. I remembered his questions about my footsteps to Virginia and the aim to earn a salute. I took count of his caution for slipping away and not making it anywhere. I considered the distant relationship we had, and yet, the letters he consistently wrote when I rarely penned a return. I thought of this valuable character in my life and the tireless way he worked to piece together our modest house and existence.

Not knowing how to leave the side of the casket, I took a deep breath, hoping to escape my tears. And as they fell from my face, I sought his approval all over again, recognizing my own stubborn disregard for his counsel. I cried and tried to calm my breath.

Knowing I had to part from him, I stepped back to stand at attention and slowly rendered Corporal Joseph Volant my salute. He deserved so much more. I wished for a moment that I did play trumpet, or that somehow, I could find the means to render Taps. I dropped my hand to my side and slowly took the white gloves from my hands. Placing the gloves neatly over his heart, I heaved again, knowing he was gone. He missed the reason, the ring, the ceremony, and all the days that would come.

Dad's main reason for not graduating to the highest order in the Knights of Columbus was the cost of a tuxedo. The Knights were associated with the Catholic Church, an organization of men that provided service in support of the church. They met monthly and taught the virtues of their purpose and allowed men to ascend through training that distinguished the four levels. Dad proudly shared his rank as a Third Degree knight, a noble position in his estimation but clearly not the highest rank.

The Knights supported their brothers and by tradition stood by the caskets of members during their wake and prior to the funeral. It was an honor guard of sorts, men dressed in tuxedos that were topped with a grand cape that had a red satin interior. Two men would stand at each end of the casket with their cape pulled back as a sign of respect and association with the Knights of Columbus. It was their duty to place the flag over Dad's casket when it was closed. They did so with precision and reverence. The knights were there to mark and honor the occasion, something that would humble even a Third Degree knight.

Riding behind the hearse with Mom, I saw the stars of the flag covering the casket through the back window, with Dad on his journey to the grave. We rode slowly through the town where he had fathered children and formed the modest life we had together. We drove to the long driveway of the church we attended for decades that began as a struggling group of young families who met weekly in a tent. I considered his stubborn criticism that the military draft made him leave the girl he loved to wear a uniform during the Korean War. And I heard his soft cadence sometimes sung as we walked together when I was young. I envisioned his faded green patrol cap, a remnant of his uniform that was occasional weekend attire. I remembered the time he took to form a concrete base for a flag pole that centered our front yard. I saw him pulling the ropes that lowered the flag on days when it was flying.

The view into the hearse was more stark, and yet, I felt the appreciation he would have had for such a symbol. Of the many ways that he would be known, few were for his fancy and none were for his fortune. But he was known for his steady duty, and the flag remembrance was such a fitting way to let him part with the honor that when called, he served.

Wheeling the casket forward to the altar, pall bearers sat at the front before the priest began the mass ceremony complete with burning incense and prayers repeated in unison. A brief reflection by the pastor referenced the younger man who was a plank holder to the church's origins, men who gathered on Saturday and set the tent up before sundown with beer. The evolution was made possible by the hardworking people, the families, and the way the community took shape.

The organ began with a familiar verse of "Amazing Grace" that was soon joined by the clarinet. It was not a campfire night and there was no polka. Instead, this instrument, never before welcomed into church liturgy, leaned heavily into the second soulful verse. The tempo of the iconic melody changed, and the clarinet mourned to the ceiling and echoed its musical lament from front to back. He played a descant and varied version of the theme, an improvisation that blew from his heart. The song was prayerful and unexpected, a powerful tribute that echoed through the cavernous church and long aisles. The player stood and slowly waved the instrument back and forth as the toll of losing his dear friend took him over. The faithful woodwind stopped short of completing the song as the soloist's gasps between tears could be softly heard.

The last song had played for Joe, the ukulele at rest, no longer requiring him to shout out the next verse and instead receiving honors in these final moments.

CHAPTER 9

Cement City

WIND BLEW ACROSS THE TARMAC with an equal dose of screams from aircraft who took off from Dharain, Saudi Arabia. After an eight-hour long flight from Germany, I was holding a greenbar printout of the manifest, a list of passengers who were arriving on the C-141 Starlifter before noon local time. The paper waved in my hand as I asked the loadmaster where the receiving party was so I could turn in our roster and move our soldiers from this stopping place to the next.

I knew the names on the list did not include Bender, we marked him absent from the bus and formation that took place before sunrise. He was an odd character, a fair soldier that took a wrong turn in his first enlistment and became a stumbling block for leaders. Prior to our notification for deployment, Bender had racked up debt, bounced several checks, and not been on time for work. After a brief period of retraining and increased supervision, it was decided he would leave the military early. He received non-judicial punishment and a loss of wages: some extra work and a route to a general discharge. But that was the plan before the unit received orders for the desert. All soldiers were to remain in place for mobilization; no retirements, no change of station, and no way home for Bender.

I had arrived at the office many hours earlier; it was New Year's

Day and our appointment to fly from Rhein-Mein Air Force Base, Germany, to somewhere in Saudi Arabia. We held a series of formations to verify that people were present and then to account for weapons issue and rations. By the time we boarded buses, I had already folded the printout into my side pocket and marked Bender absent. It was unclear to me why anyone in the Arabian Peninsula would care about the reasons for his absence. But there was speculation among the group as to where he was and how they envied his chance to spend another day somewhere else. For now, I was in pursuit of the person and office to hand over documents and load buses for the staging area.

A long line of pallets was adjacent to the group that had just landed. They were tired from extended days of training and the drain of goodbyes, formations, and the unknown. Alpha Battery's First Sergeant found a place to sit on a pallet of water bottles. He was an effective and seasoned non-commissioned officer (NCO), the top enlisted leader in his unit. The plastic wrap that secured the load had waved in the wind before he took it and converted it to his blanket. He curled up as if it were home and used the cover to shield wind; he used a gas mask that had been strapped to his side as a pillow. This was a picture, the salty and solid leader folded and succumbing to exhaustion even at this early stage. Although he did not look comfortable, it was more obvious that he had begun his journey into a new place.

Toyota trucks drove to our group, and two service members knew the arrival process and asked for the manifest. I turned it over as incomplete homework, not knowing if I needed a receipt for the transaction or if I would be graded for coming up one short. There were 139. Using their handheld radios, they called for buses that arrived thirty minutes later. We should "standby," they said, "Wait here and drink water." The buses would take us to Cement City, a place we knew nothing about that had tents and other people that just arrived. Water seemed like a decent suggestion, save for the reality that First Sergeant would have to unravel his resting spot so the others could pull through cases of bottled water. Most soldiers were looking for a place to pee instead. The long flight was a tightly fitted arrangement of strapping in along the walls of the airframe with gear at our feet prohibiting movement. The Air Force crew onboard acted disappointed to report that the wall-mounted urinal did not work. Likely, they learned that characterization after flying thousands of miles and not savoring the cleanup from bumpy flight routes.

A small group walked from the flightline to the adjacent connexes where they agreed to relieve themselves. And so, the months of living outdoors began. Where do we function? Where is a place to sit, to spit out toothpaste, and perform our daily needs? For today, it was a short walk away to a sandy berm near the long lines of connexes.

Another formation was required before we could get on the buses. One last time in ranks and in the same order to account for everyone, and Bender. I moved to each bus, asked for their count, and told the first passenger we would form one more time when we arrived. Each one agreed, but they were dull to detailed instructions at this point and wanted to finish this process and assemble with their units. One hundred thirty-nine people were from multiple artillery batteries, the units that formed our artillery battalion. There were more than five hundred men in total assigned to 2nd Battalion, 3rd Field Artillery Regiment. We were the "Gunner Battalion," a 155mm self-propelled howitzer unit that was in the Third Armored Division. We had trained for the war in Europe since my arrival. No one expected a Germany-based unit to leave for the desert. We were ready for the Fulda Gap, a location near the Czechoslovakian border where we thought the Russians were most likely to attack. We were ready for the Cold War but, instead, arrived in the desert.

We had the wrong uniforms for the desert. We had a woodland green pattern of camouflage. Units that arrived before us were issued the desert pattern called "pecan sandies." To many it seemed like a huge vulnerability, green soldiers driving green trucks with an array of slow moving tracked vehicles to include the howitzers. But for weeks we were told these obvious changes would be made. Paint for the vehicles and equipment to issue, to include new boots and uniforms.

Cement City was an hours-long bumpy ride away, a forgotten industrial site literally in the middle of nowhere, thirty minutes from Dharain, Saudi Arabia. The two-lane road that got us there was peppered by abandoned vehicles, piles of garbage, and slow rolling hills we learned were called "wadi". After the last formation and accountability as a flight manifest, soldiers were released back to unit leaders. The once napping First Sergeant now gathered his group and led them to the welcome center. Lines of soldiers weaved around the tent and along the sandy path used as a road. Leftover equipment from the concrete factory was spread out, and broken heavy equipment decorated a nearby lot. And looking into the sun, the line of tents was extensive; this was the staging area for thousands of service members deployed to Desert Shield.

My tent included the soldiers from the communications platoon and the medics. It was a forty-foot-long dingy place where metal cots had been placed and we would live until our equipment arrived. The smell of wet canvas and mildew was stagnant in the air. I took my rucksack, the sum total of three days of needs crammed into one backpack, and chose the last bunk across from my platoon sergeant. Miller was an exceptional man, a strong Christian and a professional soldier. I was grateful for him every day but especially on this first day when uncertainty and anxiety could only be solved with footsteps. He was that guy, the non-commissioned officer that led compassionately but knew the standard. He reserved his opinion and interest in officers, but he took the time to teach me and tried to steer my efforts. "It's our platoon," Miller said, with the emphasis placed on our shared ownership. Soldiers came to him with problems and he worked to solve most of those before he requested help from me. He had mastered radio repair and equipment needed to lay communications wire for artillery units in his eleven years. He was here, so he told me on day one, to make me successful. And to this point, I felt little success as a new second lieutenant but great comfort knowing my chief ally was Sergeant First Class Wade Miller.

From the day we first received an alert notice, soldiers were required to carry their gas mask. This was a two-pound rubber facemask that included an air filter system to protect against the use of chemical and biological agents. The mask fit only one way into the worn canvas pouch we strapped to our waist. It was an attempt to normalize its wear and prepare us for any combat situation with Iraq that included nerve agents. More time was spent in speculation than actual training; the Iraqis, it was broadly assumed, would fight exactly as the Russians and employ nerve gas to slow down troop movements.

In a complex of more than thirty large tents, the headquarters and dining facility was inside the huge circus tent. This was a rented piece of gear established to seat hundreds for meals and was used for training when meals were not being served. Small groups picked corners of the circus tent and trainers talked loudly and stood on tables to be heard. NBC training, the fundamentals of nuclear, biological, and chemical operations, was a recurring theme and focus. At varying intervals, the trainer would yell, "Gas! Gas! Gas!" and all the soldiers would immediately perform the drilled response. The waist-carried case snaps and Velcro opened, and the folded mask was quickly placed on our head. Target time for completion was four seconds. When the mask was fitted, the soldier placed their palms over the breathing vents and checked for leaks. After a quick inhale to validate placement, the soldier would reply, "Gas! Gas! Gas!" only with a muted and muffled tone inside the gear.

Gas mask training was a staple in the circus tent and a part of the daily routine. Trainers were in every corner evangelizing groups and rehearsing the same drill. Learning to instinctively bend over slightly to hold a helmet between the knees while placing the mask took repetitions. Four seconds seemed like a long time, but soldiers refined their skill while also looking around them to see who was not making the standard. That deficiency created the question: What will I do when I hear that alarm and my battle buddy does not have his mask on in time for protection? It was our first look into the prospect of losing someone or having them harmed by a nerve agent or other danger.

Training for NBC and first-aid had also been a part of a ramp up in Germany, except it was different now. No one had to point to realism. Atropine injections were the antidote to any nerve gas symptoms. The back pocket of the mask held two syringes, but for now, those were notional. Dummy syringes were used in training and the action of grabbing the syringe and jamming it to your buddy's thigh was merely theater. The circus tent ended that scene, and new atropine trainers were used. They squirted water that released when the pen hit the thigh with the right force. Everyone winced at the spray from the water and imagined the spring-loaded needle entering their thigh. "I'll take the nerve gas...not sure I can do the needle," was a recurring response.

In daily meetings at the reception center, word circulated that the Iraqi Army had affiliations with Russian Special Forces, or SPETSNAZ. As a result, it would be important to consider this Cement City as an area to defend against any potential attack or interest from the Iraqi military. No map was shown to describe the hundreds of miles or routes that an adversary would travel to get to us; we relied instead on the instinct to prepare for any threat. Watches and guards were posted to the perimeter of the newly formed base. Units were assigned areas and the intent was to look outward, particularly at night, and ensure that there were no such attacks.

Our battalion was assigned a large section of the perimeter and shifts were established to rotate soldiers to watch positions. In the first days, operations included creating defensive positions with sandbags and improvised equipment. Soldiers were inspired by the prospect of building and quickly found a way to hotwire an abandoned dozer to use in pushing the sand into a berm. Concrete pipes were found and moved to create an array of observation points. Wood from pallets was constructed into a funnel for sand to increase efficiency in making sandbags. Pallets were filled with sandbags and the production of our defenses grew stronger by the hour. In less than two days of continuous movement, the perimeter of Cement City was established and fully manned. And then the rain began.

Miller and I created our shift to overlap with both the night and the day hours so we could overlap with most of our soldiers. Our section of the perimeter included large concrete pipes and a foxhole dug into the high point of the berm. The rain began without lightning or thunder but continued without pause for days. Rain that was initially absorbed into the desert sand now puddled in places. The avenues and rows of tents had places where walking meant navigating around puddles. Tents in some areas needed to be reinforced so that water did not enter the sides or seep into the sleeping area. We were told and retold what items were required to include in the ruck sack: a spare set of boots, changes of socks, and even rain gear. Days into the rain season, these items were saturated, and standing post became more of a soak than repelling any onslaught or attack.

We finished our night shift after going to each position and checking in. We heard rumors about showers that may be available for the camp. We imagined they might actually have hot water and soap. Information traveled erratically, but Miller made it a point to address each report and baseline expectations. He encouraged rest knowing that even in the less than two weeks we had been "in country," a physical tax had been levied and was exaggerated when drenched. We walked into the dark tent, passed the medics, passed each squad until our parking spot. Exhausted, I peeled my boots off and set the wet socks on the end of the cot. Soon I was inside a damp sleeping bag, sequestered from the ongoing storm and the duties of that day.

Awakening to morning light creeping into the front, I dug for the next pair of almost dry socks and the alternate boots. The uniform was in shambles at this point, but I needed to get to the daily meeting with the commander and held my gear in hand, moving to the front tent flap. I passed a mix of sleeping and awake platoon members and the medics who shared our dank space. Staff Sergeant Coverson pulled the flap before I got to the front and passed me with a question I did not hear. I stepped through the exit of the tent before turning back to get him to repeat his inquiry. The front bunk at the entrance was Private

First Class Morgan, a thin and shy medic from Pittsburgh. He was new to the Army and had arrived in Germany only two months before we left for another continent. He seemed uncertain about his place with the medics and even less sure about this military life. Turning back from the front, the flap was open and cast light on the figure of Morgan sitting in his bunk, slumped, with his helmet and gear in a pile at his feet.

Coverson's question was repeated, but I missed hearing it again as my focus shifted to Morgan, his face spotted and staring at his hands planted on his knees. He was leaned over too far to be comfortable and did not move with the action at the front of the tent. I waited and expected him to return my look, but he was still and fixed. It was then that I saw his t-shirt was also spotted and blotched in an irregular pattern. Concerned, I stepped back in to sit on his bunk and examine Morgan closer and understand.

Miller burst into the front and quickly spotted me next to our medic. The tent flap opened fully with his appearance shedding another flash of light on the slouching medic. Miller's voice commenced in a staccato report and described the soldiers from Alpha Battery whose sandbag-fortified position collapsed last night. Sergeant Tracy Hampton was inside the two-person outlook in a bunker structured with wood and overlaid with sandbags. He and his younger Soldier Hayes had been in this position since it was first established, adding new bags and improving it during the days of ongoing rain. But last night they were satisfied that their defensive position was complete. Hayes stood at the entrance to the bunker and was headed for more sandbags when Hampton asked him to wait from inside. They could pause for now; and so, the soldier followed his direction and stood at the entrance to their newly announced completed position.

When the wood snapped, more than five layers of bags landed on Hampton. The collapse covered him immediately with broken timber, and in that instant, the remainder of the position crumbled. Hayes immediately pulled the bags away while screaming, injured by falling material and horrified that his leader was crushed under layers of wood and soaked, heavy sandbags. The digging began and his frantic yells for assistance were answered by other Alpha Battery soldiers who pulled, lifted, and called for medics.

Baumholder and his crew from Alpha Battery were the first to hear the odd call from the fallen bunker. Hayes was pressed into the ground by hundreds of pounds of sand and debris, compressing his lungs and making him incapable of loud screaming. Instead, a high trumpeting sound blew into the sunrise as Hayes squirmed and tried to signal for help. Baumholder's crew paused to hear it and then were in a footrace to the collapse. Troubled by the unnatural sound and trying to interpret its meaning, they arrived together and dove into the bunker to wrestle apart the broken pieces.

Yells for additional help notified anyone within hearing distance that help was required. Baumholder's team pulled bags and slung them to the side, joined by others in a bucket-line to disassemble the fallen bunker. With no shovel, they used their hands to move sand, all the while hoping to find Hampton. They could see Hayes in his covered position, still bearing the weight and providing short phrases with details of what happened. Soldiers furiously took apart the heavy pieces, throwing sand from every side.

Morgan and another medic were positioned near the center of our assigned perimeter, and quick footsteps led him to the crumbled scene. Doc, our newly assigned physician's assistant, was in a tent that others ran into to alert him to the urgent need. For now, Morgan and his sergeant were first to the bunker with the stretcher and joined their medic bag adjacent to Hampton and the flurry of Alpha Battery soldiers. By then, they had an opened space and could see his contorted body and head turned to their faces.

With little light and drizzling rain, the medics provided urgent care, quickly opening his airway and beginning compressions. Broken and sharp wood cut Hampton, and sandbags dented his body. Surrounding soldiers continued to pull the debris away and another yelled that a helicopter transport was requested and "dust off" would soon arrive. The sergeant directed the group nearby to unfold the stretcher, and frantically, Atkinson pointed to four of his strongest and told them they would carry the litter.

Morgan heaved over Hampton with compressions to his sternum and compulsively stopped to listen for breath, then pushed his own into his mouth again and again. Thin but tireless, Morgan kept the sets and pace for more than thirty minutes, an exhausting burst of energy in his first test of crisis response. As Hampton's response was waning, Morgan became more intense in his activity, pushing deeper breaths into his mouth, pressing more deliberately into his broken chest. Injuries to his abdomen had erupted and created discharge of blood clots and fluid with each push. Another round of yelling ensued as Doc arrived and gave the location and time for evacuation. Morgan joined the others in lifting Hampton's listless body onto the stretcher and, with his last contact to his first patient, pulled his arm to his side. They ran unevenly through the puddles and around barriers to load the Black Hawk helicopter.

Morgan remained at the spoiled and broken position, not knowing whether to join the others in piecing together the remnants or to grab his medic bag and depart. Atkinson barked at him to get his gear and return to headquarters, and Morgan was defeated, breathless and without words, as he got up and roamed back to the tent. The sun was not up and the night was not over, but the day, the day Tracy Hampton died, was forever etched into our newest medic.

When I touched Morgan's shoulder in the tent, he turned his head to me without making eye contact. I moved closer, and the odd sweet odor from his shirt made me reconsider the blotches in his face and shirt. He mumbled when I began to ask if he was okay when Miller sat on his other side. It was Miller's hand on his shoulder that broke the dam of Morgan's emotions. He shivered and wept, his words heaving in every burst. Miller pulled him in closely and firmly, trying to absorb his quivering and listen to the erratic voice and a stream of reports that "it did not work." The dried blood and dirt rubbed into their embrace.

Three days later, the rain stopped without a sun to offer contrast or dry the puddles, pools, and streams formed by more than a week of rain. Tents that were ruined with water and pressing winds were replaced, and a new tent was erected and left empty. Chairs from the circus tent were moved to this impromptu chapel created for a ceremony. There would only be chairs for Hampton's platoon, the smaller group of Alpha Battery soldiers, with his crew of five sitting up front. There was no announcement of the memorial service, and yet, everyone knew it would happen, and on that morning made their way to the crowded tent.

Standing at the back, the tent roofline sagged downward and made it difficult for everyone to stand up straight. We held our helmets in our hands, crowded next to one another, and moved in silence to a place and moment we did not expect. The chaplain, a tall black man from the brigade headquarters, interrupted the blankness with words of scripture. Difficult to hear, he turned from side to side and tried to allow everyone to understand his words. He pointed to First Lieutenant Kenneth Jones who moved forward. Kenny was Hampton's platoon leader and a stout man with immeasurable strength. He spoke with a passion about regular things on normal days, but this morning his booming voice filled the tent. "Yea, though I walk through the valley of the shadow of death," began his exhortation. His voice worked without tremble and was steady in this moment, a grace bestowed upon him by his own beliefs and calling in life.

First Lieutenant Kenneth Jones.

The wind that had come when the rain stopped accelerated and pushed on the mounting of the newly set up chapel tent. Strong gusts slapped at the flaps, and the air exchange forced the roof to dip and pull down. The roof canvas flexed downward, forcing my head down. And again, Kenny spoke to the group. Almost in response, the wind blew again, pushing my head down and making it easier for tears to move from my face. Kenny paused and turned his head to look across the gathering place. Savoring the silence, he pointed to the boots placed together and the rifle standing up with Hampton's helmet. He paid tribute to our brother and said he would be forever remembered. Standing for the close of the somber gathering, we stood to salute. Soldiers from Jones' platoon were up front, their hands and arms still aching from their heroic effort. Taps played, and their weary arms moved back to the side.

Among the seventeen lieutenants of the "Gunner Battalion," Kenny was more senior by months and had other experience we all lacked. But that day, he also had strength beyond that we knew; he shared wisdom we thirsted for in a moment of darkness. He asked us all, "What is this life, if not for the glory of God? Something that Tracy Hampton knew." Kenny secured his revered place by rising above what he saw and calling us to look onward.

Captain Bledsoe was the fire direction officer, a technical position where all the computer systems fed into his vehicle to compute the range, target, and ammunition required for the battalion. Each battery had its own subset of his computer system, each artillery piece had a read-out of the calculations and adjustments needed to precisely hit targets twenty-two kilometers away. With rocket assisted munitions, called "copperhead," the guns could reach thirty kilometers. Bledsoe leveraged this role to his advantage. He ran high-level training and through repetition had impacted the readiness and effectiveness of the unit. He was rightly paired with the expert senior enlisted advisor, Master Sergeant Marks, an exceptionally tall and imposing figure whose word was rarely challenged. As a result of Bledsoe's successes, he gave himself latitude to philosophize on our current situation and his estimate of how this war would be fought. He had a bully pulpit and a teammate that beamed credibility.

Bledsoe fancied himself as an appreciated comedian, a role he never earned despite his own unrelenting attempts to be funny. The intermittent comedy was in his exaggeration and the comedian who tried harder and became more brash to get the laugh points. Perhaps it was because of this disparity that we listened more intently to his predictions and theories of what would happen next. Perhaps what he lacked in comedic value was offset by his insights into warfare. We took solace in his comments that our green camouflage uniforms were not actually a liability. Indeed, by his measure, the Iraqi Republican Guard likely feared "green guys" because they knew, at least by his report, the armored divisions of the United States were extremely capable. He put a finer point on that by adding that when the Iraqis saw "Spearhead," the words above our division patch, they would be further intimidated, likening it to General George Patton in World War II.

No one questioned his accumulation of facts, and few considered if the Iraqis could read English or understand Western history from fifty years ago. Instead, we took confidence from Bledsoe. It was not comforting to hear that more blood would be shed, but Captain Bledsoe made that prediction days after the memorial. We took it in soberly, and then wished he was instead offering portions of his satirical verse.

Road systems were created by large diesel fuel trucks that were equipped with sprayers attached to the rear with dozens of small nozzles. Routes were created when they sprayed diesel into the sand with two large trucks traveling together. Although there was some evaporation, eventually enough fuel soaked into the sand to form a surface that became the road system. Navigation was possible by oil barrels that were spray painted different colors. The barrel became markers along the side of roads. Our battalion traveled on yellow barrel road to our staging area, a two-days' drive from Cement City.

Departing from the barrel road, we formed a single file line of vehicles weaving across miles of undisturbed sand. There were bumps that shook the vehicle and changes in the tilt and angle that made us list from side to side. Maps and loose items placed in the vehicle fell and stirred to the floor and seats. If it was not tied down, the bumps and turns shifted it. Small changes in the topography were called wadi, gentle slopes that gave depth to the long view of the endless desert. Passing the crest of the wadi, a donkey and camels were visible. A young boy was nearby, walking with the pack and turning his head to discover the land invasion of noisy trucks, armored personnel carriers, and tracked vehicles. The animals moved without disturbance and were more interested in small bushes or grass where they could feed. He waved slowly when my vehicle passed him, a blank face with a dirty but colorful outer garment covering his long white robe and pants.

Headquarters battery occupied an open space more than a quarter mile across. Bulldozers pushed sand around the edges to make an imperfect circle, and we parked our vehicles inside like minute marks on a clock's face. Over the coming days, a series of meetings covered the hours and our routine in this distant landscape came together. Before sunlight each morning, we awoke to "stand to," the time to look outward from our positions on the berm and observe any activity, a key time for leaders to update information and prepare reports.

The SPETSNAZ that were expected in Cement City never appeared, but the Iraqis had been effective in their use of SCUD missiles. Each reported launch was announced on the radio, "SCUD, SCUD, SCUD!" and because chemical weapons were expected, the response required everyone to put on their gas mask for protection. This occurrence grew to be normal and a battery-operated alarm, the M8, was kept outside the headquarters to detect chemical use.

At an overnight stop en route to our location, the radio squealed with the SCUD report, scrambling soldiers to grab their gear and respond. One NCO ran to the others screaming for his mask and was without it, desperate for help. In an instant, the professional person who had more than a dozen years in uniform, and responsibility for dozens more soldiers, was without the primary item of our recurring training. The canvas case and mask served as his pillow that evening, but in the flurry of the alarm response, his comfort piece was pushed away and out of reach. His seniority evaporated with this loss. His panic peaked and his screams turned to sobs crying for his mask. Others looked alongside him, retracing his route to the group and eventually coming back to the vehicle where he slept. Voices from the volunteers who helped were muffled in stark contrast to his plea with an uncovered face.

Captain Tiergan was an extremely bright artillery officer who commanded the headquarters battery and was my direct supervisor. I found him heartless and stale as a leader but followed his consistently correct direction, particularly now when the stakes seemed high. In following his direction, I learned the value of silence but was torn for my own want to add a human dimension to the tasks we completed. Each one could be a chance to listen to our soldiers and cheer their development. This was their first time in combat, their first trip with an unknown date of return. I knew they wanted more information and felt extremely separated from our purpose and any perspective other than the banal daily facts. As a newly branded first lieutenant, my own zeal to perform was centered on advocating. From my enlistment at age 17 and then four years of college, it had been almost eight years since I first put on the uniform.

Oddly, the time in service seemed more like a patchwork of experiences, each one suggesting another necessary step or rung in the ladder. With each evolution, I believed that the next step, the next promotion, or the achievement of one goal would satisfy a hunger to exorcize my dark secret. The elimination of my secret and dented past was over the horizon, or so I thought. Enlisting was a way to escape the geography and reset the scene from my childhood. College was something that I saw as a needed step to rebrand my character and provide evidence. With a commission, despite Dad's misgivings, I would transcend the feelings of incompleteness and have a way to fill the hole. Imagination and fear of being discovered were a fuel for new challenges that ended without satisfaction.

Tiergan was unrelenting in his taskings, sending me to account for equipment in every section that had been checked almost daily before we left Germany. The repetition appeared as a solution to vacant time and a requirement that delivered no value. Soldiers, in my estimation, wanted something more than inventories to consume their day. Miller helped develop refresher training on our machine guns and the tactical tasks to support our defense. Tiergan created an argument for foot patrols that drew interest from the battalion headquarters; we should form them tomorrow and begin a program of marches into the night to secure our perimeter.

McKinley Burke served as the senior communications expert for the battalion. He had more than twenty years of service and his last assignment was as an instructor at the Army's radio school. He knew tactical radios and all the associated equipment that enabled radios to connect computers to each gun. Soldiers provided input for targets for command and control. But without the radios, and without Burke to oversee their use and readiness, there were no missions. He balanced this revered position carefully, using it to argue for resources or to inspire younger soldiers to learn from his able hand. He was considered a bit of a gray beard with sage advice and calm resolve when others were confused.

SCUD missiles were an enduring threat and a weapon that was least understood by our headquarters. Radio alerts were sent when radar detected a missile launch, but the notice only identified that a SCUD was in the air and no details were known about its intended target. As a result, "SCUD, SCUD, SCUD!" interrupted routine radio traffic causing everyone to immediately move to a bunker or fighting position to take cover. It was a drill that was repeated without pattern almost daily.

Small tents could fit three people if needed, but I shared a GP Small with Sergeant Haskins. The design made it appear like an Indian teepee with added side connections to make it bigger. But not much bigger. One person could stand at its center with a wooden pole that peaked the decades-old canvas. After a patrol and late evening of waiting for their return, I landed in the cot, a metal frame that held a nylon cover, and dozed off in minutes.

Almost like a regular clock alarm, the M8, a nuclear, biological, and chemical alarm, could be heard sending its emergency code. Screaming interrupted scarce moments of rest, and I was startled by the SCUD report. Haskins was quick with his rifle and exited our modest resting place and joined the repetition of "SCUD!" so that the message would pass down the line. I reached for my pistol and pulled my pants up. With boots pulled on and helmet placed on my head, I bumped through the front flap on the tent and moved to the direction of our sand hole firing position. I was late to escape the GP Small's front flap and began to race. Darkness and confusion covered me as my foot caught the corner rope tiedown, causing me to fall and land flat in the sand.

Pain in my ankle sparked through my leg as I moved to recover and realized I was tangled in the loose rope. Each position yelled directions and began their reporting of who was safe in their hole. The M8 continued to alarm. My ankle seemed to buzz with pain and my heart rate sped with each moment I glared at the blur of activity. I attempted to crawl while the names and numbers passed from one to the other. No radios or wire connected our foxholes; Burke moved information by foot. Ears ringing, the night went into slow motion as panic took over my response. Burke was crouched over, moving from the end of the line, securing the reports and confirming that we were all in the right spot.

As I saw his dark face over me, words were lost, and I groaned as I tried again to move my legs and get up. Without pause, Burke glared at me, his eyes cutting into my fears and confusion. Life went into slow motion. His strong arm reached to me and his loud, low voice commanded, "On me." His eyes turned their focus from my face to my arm when his calm resolve caused him to nod his head in affirmation. I understood his intent immediately, to pull me up, but was still dull to movement before he yelled it more intensely, "On me!" His fingers wrapped my wrist tightly. My hand lifted to grab his arm in response, and his strong pull nearly slung me into the dug out sand hole ten feet from where I had fallen.

Burke was gone and moving to the end of the platoon before I absorbed what had really happened. I had fallen, tripped by a rope and paralyzed by my fear. Burke made no notice of the crumbled spirit of his new lieutenant; he reached his arm to me in an unexpected rescue. I stared outward from our perimeter, my foot tingling and my heart slowing from the terror that followed the alarm. Haskins was quiet now and intently searching the sky for missiles or activity. Looking to the stars, I saw the blinking lights of aircraft, a common occurrence when planes flew overhead to refuel aircraft sorties.

Rehearsals was the name given to convoys and vehicle movements that we practiced for days. The self-propelled howitzers, armored vehicles, fuel trucks, ammunition carriers, and Humvees were arranged across an open swath of the desert. We moved from the circle formation and spread the vehicles out like geese following their lead. Winding formations moved to the direction of our headquarters and to known points given by radio command. Rehearsals were a reality check for the way vehicles were prepared and packed. If items were loose, the roll and pitch of the desert as we traveled made them break and fall from truck beds. There wasn't room enough for the required gear, and the twelve-mile-per-hour pace of the battalion weaned everyone from what was not essential.

Windshields were removed from trucks where possible, a requirement derived from the fear that breaking glass in combat operations would injure passengers. With continued rain and strong winds, slow movement soaked and wore down drivers. The landscape seemed forever the same and shapeless, without known points to navigate from or desert features that looked different. Over time, drivers learned how to pace themselves to follow at the right interval and avoid dramatic changes in speed. It was a monotonous existence, leaving in darkness to conduct rehearsals and returning late in the day to refuel and recharge for the next day. Everything fit into a routine, including the food rations that consisted of canned Chef Boyardee lunch cups boiled in water for lunch and tray rations that were all chicken breast in gravy. The days of the week blended together as well, and soon it was all repeatable and unchanging.

73 EASTING

At a routine meeting at the end of one day's training, Tiergan told me that tomorrow we were leaving our circle berm and now safe perimeter. Rehearsals that stretched vehicles across the horizon would now lead us across the border into Iraq. Traveling down the line of vehicles to share the news face to face, I grew more aware of its meaning with each acknowledgement for soldiers. They signaled the strongest desire to move forward and to get on with whatever was next, ignoring any risk and opting instead simply for change. They foraged for the last packs of ramen noodles hidden in boxes from Germany and prepared a celebratory meal.

Night patrols had bonded our platoon and gave them fellowship away from the tedious perimeter and the quiet watch. Two machine guns were assigned to the platoon, and they carried it with them and rotated the person to carry. In carrying out this routine task, younger soldiers were taught how to disassemble the weapon. Their proficiency grew quickly until it was an evening contest before heading out into the darkness. Who could hold the machine gun, ground it, disassemble it into the rain poncho, and then reassemble the entire weapon? The competition drew yells from most and encouragement only from the other new soldiers. The final check in reassembly was to pull the bolt back before pulling the trigger to hear a click, confirming correct performance. Haskins placed himself as the arbiter of both time and completeness. But without a stopwatch, the group took his official report as he attempted to stare at his wristwatch and translate his second hand reading. It was largely inaccurate, done by flashlight and prone to his own favoritism and grudges.

As a communications officer, I had a printed copy of the radio channels for all the units in the brigade. We routinely tuned into our own battalion traffic to understand what was currently happening and to try to figure out what was next. But long hours in rehearsals had taught us to tune to other channels when nothing was coming through on our own radio. We listened to the higher command or adjacent units. We learned about the refuel plans from channels dedicated to those messages. Over time, we memorized our playlist and could quickly shift from one channel to the next in order to keep our updates and interest fresh.

The Battle of 73 Easting, what we knew as "another day," was just a planned route to divert the Iraqi Republican Guard that aimed to defeat them from their rear lines. Few anticipated it would be the resounding success or defining moment in armored tank conflict. The deception plan, to make the Iraqis look to their front while we approached from the rear, conceived of at a higher headquarters, did not get shared down at the user level. Sitting in a Humvee next to Miller, we simply followed the trail of vehicles to our front, reported fuel levels, and looked across the horizon. Daylight departures turned to night, and we moved with deliberate but slow pace, eventually crossing a substantial berm and high place that we knew was the border to Kuwait.

Abandoned holes and firing positions, improvised bunkers made from blocks and sand, were strewn across the horizon. Smoke rose in the distance, the first evidence that Saddam Hussein had set fire to the Ramadi oil fields, an attempt to cause environmental damage. Looking to our left and right, we saw the battalion stretch out like the pattern of geese flying in formation. Except that we were not nearly as elegant, going over bumps and passing heaps of trash left behind. Old buildings that were once a border station were riveted with bullet holes. The radio began to churn orders and reports confirming vehicles and locations. Miller and I spun through our playlist to get the right information and tune into where decisions were being made. A refuel point was planned ahead, but the idea of pausing seemed to work against what we saw as a beginning to combat operations.

As the night came, our battalion had weaved through miles and an A-10 "Warthog" circled overhead, directed by the Air Force to hit tanks in the open. We found the channel for coordination and watched the maverick missiles launch from the side, leaving a pink trail before hitting the turret of the T-72 tank. In the darkness, the explosion provided light enough to see people escaping from the burning vehicles, tumbling from the concussion in a bright flash. With night vision goggles, we looked into the distance and saw fires and moving vehicles made clear by the green and sparkling background. When hit, the turret flipped like a coin thrown in the air and secondary explosions from ammunition made a resounding boom. TOW missiles fired from Bradley Fighting Vehicles launched to hit enemy tanks and were steered by small rockets that corrected its direction. The blast from firing the TOW was followed by fast increments of short blasts like maracas rhythmically firing and leading the missile to its intended target. Explosions lit the horizon with fire that appeared white in the goggles, making small bodies and parts appear before a stage curtain.

The three batteries of artillery from our unit were supported by two additional artillery battalions. When we crossed the border into Kuwait, the Multiple Launch Rocket System (MLRS) battalion was added to our formation. We paused at varying intervals for fire missions, requests to destroy enemy vehicles and positions that were five to eight kilometers to our front. For simplicity and maximum effect, each mission was a "battalion three" and every gun fired three times at every identified target. Bledsoe's system computed the requirements that were dialed into each gun with precision, allowing all the rounds to land in a flurry. In total, each target was hit by eighty-one rounds, easily destroying groups of trucks and soldiers targeted in the open.

We moved three times during the night, and with each pause, completed more fire missions. Miller and I roamed through radio channels, each churning with activity and reports. As morning light first came to the horizon, my platoon was arrayed in a circle adjacent to the fire direction center. A morning status report was due soon, and I made my way to each vehicle to see faces and gather information. Days before we crossed the border, rest was interrupted with tasks, leaving sleep into an unpredictable period of slouch in the truck or infrequent chance to lay on the hood. The pattern of changing socks or having coffee in the morning eroded into a persistent dullness from the lack of rest. The terrain was far more uneven, and I was disoriented on seeing the complete circle of trucks. I turned to see where I started and looked for a moment at the towering fire direction van, a five-ton truck with a metal connex containing antennas, computers, and experts who sent the digital messages that were the essence of fire missions.

Having parked in darkness, the straight lines and alignment of the formation had evaporated. Confused, I looked for Tiergan's vehicle knowing I could recognize it as the one sand-colored vehicle in our battery. He had arranged for his truck to run through the spray booth in Saudi Arabia but was surprised when no one envied the paint or his privilege. Poor light made it harder to orient, and I stepped to a higher mole to conduct a visual survey. The back door of the FDC van burst open, Master Sergeant Marks turning to the stairs. Alarmed by the door slamming as it blew open, I looked to his direction, a white flash covered the horizon and illuminated the sky. More flashes came. A violent boom deafened me. The scene went black and white.

My head pulled back in response and the thunderous concussion thumped my unstable body. Traveling at Mach speed, the MLRS rocket sounded an explosion that I felt in the chest and rang through my ears. My eyes squinted at the flashing light and the ringing took over all sounds. Feeling my body fly into a star, my heart raced as I dove into a nearby pit, rolling over my rifle and twisting my helmet. My eyes only saw sparkles with vision that was without focus, with my heart racing spinning me into a fetal position. Follow-on explosions came from nearby guns of the battalion in a thunderous tirade of artillery unleashed on targets.

My ears were unable to take in screaming from Marks, now moving toward me as I wrestled to a stop. Marks was made taller by his silhouette created by more explosions and artillery firing. Smoke and the pungent stench of sulfur rolled over the tilted landscape. Trails of smoke surrounded his slow-motion movements. Seeing him above me seemed to stop time. My mouth filled with sand as I tossed myself into hiding, feeling my body leave reality and being covered with fear. My eyes were squinted and unclear, seeing the now brilliant light of additional guns firing. He arrived at the edge, still yelling and now smiling as he saw my foolish collapse when I imagined incoming enemy fire. I saw more than one image as the mosaic of vision changed with each blink.

My ear ringing was loud and dizzying my perception of the scene. His finger pointed behind us to the other guns nearby, and I took in the magnitude of my miscalculation. I shook my head trying to restore my focus, but as I stared into Marks and the smoking backdrop, I saw more dots and streaks. I reached my hands to my head to straighten my helmet and brush sand from my cheeks. My audition for combat had failed. We had rehearsed, trained, and been taught the responses to each action. I saw that moment and knew I had no control over it, and no way to undo my perception that we were being attacked.

Humbled, I rose slowly and reached for the rifle that left my side in the pit. I pulled my flak vest together at the seam and pulled at my waist to align my pistol with my left side and my mask on the right. In a moment of intensity, my test for steadiness had collapsed into a shallow hole, and the finger of certainty pointed into my miss. I considered the many steps leading to this day, the one where I would be battle tested. I knew the record would not outshine my own sadness or the stains from being touched. The experience of combat held no power to remove the tattoo. I reconsidered the event over time and saw the incomplete nature of proving or establishing courage in such a moment. There was only instinct, the things your body did naturally as a result of training and a will to live.

CHAPTER 10

Next to Roster 31

THE PACKING LIST WAS THE sole requirement that did not include motion. Air Assault School was a rigorous two weeks of movement, being tested and learning the basics of rappelling from heights. The packing list detailed all the items that were inspected on the first day and included all the gear issued to every soldier. From the canteen to the wet-weather jacket, the items totaled more than forty pounds that fit tightly into a medium-sized rucksack.

The inspection was the second element of Zero Day, the test that determined who could participate in the actual course. Beginning with a 0400 show time, all of the people that were scheduled for the course arrived and directed to find a seat in a large metal building. As evidence that it would be a demanding week, instructors were positioned throughout the darkness leading to the meeting place and were actively yelling at those who moved without intention.

Shuffling from the parking lot, too many were surprised by the instructors, dressed in pressed camouflage uniforms with creased black hats. Each of them had mastered the techniques of the Air Assault Course, and by their commands to the unwashed new arrivals, they stood as exemplars of soldiers and exacting teachers. They barked orders and yelled at slow movers to drop for push-ups. They grilled them and taxed their morning.

Afraid of heights from youth, I took the challenge of Air Assault School weeks earlier, recognizing that Zero Day was not the opportune time to overcome my long-held fear. Other officers from my unit graced me with sessions on the obstacle course, filled with elaborate instructions on how to complete each one. They were not the toughest obstacles in the Army, but they tested strength and confidence to overcome fears. Each had a nickname highlighting its purpose or most famous attribute. They were made more difficult because of the journey in darkness to the metal building, each round of push-ups depleting strength preserved for the obstacle course.

Many struggled with the Dirty Name, an obstacle that required three logs to be crossed, each one at a different height. The first could be stepped on, and the remaining two made you lean forward and leap to grab the next higher log. There was no graceful way to overcome the logs. Jumping from one to another required absorbing the ascension in the abdomen and then quickly hugging the log for stability. Using a three-point stance, the soldier then rose to jump to the next rung. Finally at its peak, the exit of the obstacle required the strength to suspend yourself before letting go or simply falling to the ground. The Dirty Name efficiently eliminated many who underestimated the complexity of three simple but separated logs.

The hardest for me was the Confidence Climb, a forty-foot-tall ladder also constructed from logs. From the first rung to the top, each of ten logs was farther apart, requiring an ability to achieve a three-point stance on each. By the top of the ladder, the reach to the next rung was above chest level so that a person needed to pull themselves up and over the log. The ladder was taxing physically, but for a person overcome with fear, the challenge was focusing on the steps and not the height.

Having worked on a helicopter for two years when I first joined the Army, I might have acclimated to the view of heights from a side window. Lining up with a main and reserve parachute strapped on might have exposed me to heights and the frenzied exit into darkness.

My mind focused instead on my current challenge and the truth that an eighteen-year-old boy takes chances at a rate and pace substantially different than a man in his thirties.

Although there were sides to the obstacle, successful completion of the Confidence Climb did not allow use of the sides and required consistent progress. Those who were frozen by fear or exhaustion were eliminated. And then they needed to climb down.

My preview of the course and the obstacles proved useful when the sun began to rise and we were called from the metal building to make our start. Shamefully, my course mentors had missed detailing the arrival process for Zero Day and later chuckled at my retelling of parking lot madness and the iterations of push-ups that I completed before arriving at my seat.

Rank and uniform decorations were not allowed for students. No protocol or perception of status would override the black hat's dominance and lead role. Instead, they marked each student with a roster number that began with "E" for enlisted service members or "O" for officers. After completing the requirements for Zero Day, numbers were sprayed on masking tape, providing our two-week moniker simply by who had met the initial objective. Mine was O32, a title rebranded using the phonetic Oscar Three Two.

Assigned to a platoon of other student service members, we were a collection of numbers standing next to one another. There were mostly Army guys, but the other services had attendees too, albeit equally homogenized by the naming convention. Echo Three One stood to my left in ranks. He was a corporal from an infantry battalion, a strong and highly motivated example of our nation's finest and an intensely physical specimen. I was assigned as his battle buddy, an inseparable partnership made from our numerical proximity and nothing more.

The first week of training was deeply technical, requiring memorization of aircraft characteristics and air assault operations. In late August, the chance to be inside the metal building should have been an oasis, but early morning starts and the drain of physical activities made not falling asleep more difficult than digesting the course material. We took notes, responded to instructor questions with classroom unison, and accumulated a set of note cards to study. Three One and I stood next to one another in hourly rest breaks and reviewed the cards. His physical stature and strength outsized his capacity for learning the material.

Stimulating intellect was not the primary goal of the Black Hats who circled our formation and training looking for deviations to punish. "Beat your boots!" screeched from each of them as they identified an error or misstep. The exercise required twenty repetitions of lowering the body and keeping a straight back to slap the sides of boots. It was an odd and common activity in the training area. Those who slept in class, whose uniform was not straight, and who did not abide by each demand were destined for this up-and-down routine.

After the first time Three One failed the Week One test, I was invited to join him for the extracurricular beating boots session. We also shared a potentially optional invitation for a study session to review the cards and memorize the material. And beat boots. We studied helicopter lift capacities, landing signals for aircraft, and requirements for air assault operations. By the end of Week One, to include the turbulence of Zero Day, the class was smaller by one third. Less than half completed the course.

Week Two continued with longer days and physical training that began before sunrise. The run distance increased and the August heat rendered us spent when the day was finished. Three One and I tied knots together and learned the configuration for rigging heavy loads that could be carried by helicopters to various locations. Large five-hundred-gallon rubber bladders holding water, called Blivets, were a common item for aerial resupply. Humvee trucks and artillery pieces could be carried as well. Each had a required set of rigging and straps that kept the load intact and allowed it to be clipped to the hook of a helicopter. We learned to inspect the loads, tie the knots, and experience pick up from rotary wing aircraft. Three One and I were well matched in this area, learning the knots and moving quickly from piece to piece to inspect the load.

Connected to two ropes, a carabiner secured at our waist linked to a rope seat we formed and tied repeatedly. There was one way to tie it. The Black Hat screamed the instructions and steps. Those few who tied it another way went home. Three One and I celebrated this milestone together knowing this allowed us to rappel from platforms used in the course. Just when I believed the repetition of tying the knot was too much, so too was the rappel descent from three towers. He and I completed the circuit, untied and re-tied the seat, and then stood in line to do it all over again.

After the traditional rappel was completed, a morning demonstration brought a helicopter near the training area, and ten soldiers slid down a rope in rapid succession. This was the Fast Rope, a three-inch-wide cotton rope simply gripped by hands and feet to allow descent. Use of this technique was common in special operations and allowed insertion of troops on rooftops or locations in seconds. Two or three soldiers could fast rope simultaneously, requiring only ten feet between descending troops.

The demonstration was inspiring, and Three One seemed both amazed and highly motivated. My perception was more cautious, expecting that this high-speed maneuver would require another round of instruction, repetition, and circuits to master the fast rope. I grossly overestimated the time allotted. We quickly lined up to a thirty-foot tower, and after one descent, stood in the next line to board the aircraft.

Echo Three One grinned as we had made it to the line and next phase. In moments, we would board the helicopter and repeat the tower activity from eighty feet above the ground. This was his destination for the entire course. The fear of heights I had suppressed to this point was still present and likely increased knowing that acclimation to the rope was not included.

The Black Hats took notice of Three One, finding his spark and grin deserving of a session to beat boots. We paired to complete them and then returned to the line. More grins and yells that "Yes, Sergeant, Air Assault," he was highly motivated. Beat boots again.

Boarding the helicopter from the side, we leaned forward and lowered our heads to run and jump to the open floor. The Black Hawk helicopter engines whined, and we pitched forward to quickly lift from the ground and circle the nearby field. Looking to the aircraft crew chief at the center, he pushed the rolled-up rope hooked to a steel arm that swiveled outside the door. Verbal commands from the Black Hat competed with the engine's sounds and strong wind blowing through the cabin. I stared into the instructor, attempting to understand the direction, and saw Three One keenly focused with stern jaw. Sweat from my palms was not dried by the breeze and my black leather gloves were not tight enough.

Exiting by the Fast Rope was a leap of faith requiring the soldier to push from the helicopter and simply grab the rope with hands and then curl feet around its three-inch width. No safety rope, no carabiner, no seat tied to our torso. Leap, and grab it. Tighter grip by hands or feet slowed descent. Simple. But the start was non-negotiable.

Barking that we were near the place where the Black Hawk would hover, the Black Hat turned his head to blast ten soldiers with the important command, "Look to the horizon." The urgency of this moment arrived as we were clear to exit.

Spinning from the intensity of this moment, I vibrated with rapid fire questions in my head blowing like the strong wind through the cabin. Was this really going to happen? Was there a green light like I had seen years before in parachute operations? Why was this rope made of cotton? Why was the rope not made from something strong like Kevlar? How could it be that my leather gloves were the sole anchor to this dangling rope? Was the rope actually touching the ground? Why had we spent so much time beating boots and so little time experiencing gravity on the Fast Rope? What is the physics of a 172-pound man descending to Earth?

Seeing the first soldier ready his feet to the side of the aircraft,

I glanced again at Three One. The grin reappeared, unscathed by the danger I felt and the punishment meant to extinguish his joy while we waited. He turned his eyes to me, giving his loudest exclamation, "Isn't this beautiful, man?" I thought of hack movie scripts and phrases repeated from military movies that seemed overblown and artificial. And then he turned to go before me, slapping my back in rigorous encouragement.

Rolling from the rope when I landed safely, it seemed like a furious dream made up of my biggest fears and completed with greatest satisfaction. Three One moved to my side, and we ran together to the Black Hat directing us to sit and watch the remainder fall to the ground, dangling by a cotton rope. Some leaned back and twirled in descent. The rotor wash from the helicopter blew dust in our faces, and I wiped it away, feeling my emotions rise.

Three One was both unblemished and undisturbed from his joy in acting the part of professional soldier. It was his life's work and sole purpose. He saw beyond the questions I asked as a man in my thirties and more in tune with my mortality. Fearless and dedicated, E31 inspired me to look beyond earthly limitations and the fear that captured my past. Indeed, he could "look to the horizon" to accomplish goals and complete the mission.

On the last day of Air Assault, we started early again, now wearing the rucksack and all the items inspected at the beginning. Tired and worn by the demands of the course, twelve more miles measured those who could finally wear the badge of completion. Three One and I paced one another, leaning forward as the sun rose to simply get the next step. Slow hills were matched by increasing heat and unlimited sweating. Blisters on the feet were only seen later, the key was to have momentum where required to accomplish the task.

Our pairing seemed fortuitous. We mumbled encouragement in the foot march and kept a steady pace behind the leader. I tuned out the physicality and thought of the finish line. I marveled at our team of two making it through the torment and the tyranny of my fears. I absorbed his grin and motivation. Mentors from my unit were there for the pinning. I introduced E31 as a trophy and catalyst for strength.

The weather soon cooled in the evenings, welcoming fall and increased unit readiness. I was assigned to an infantry brigade, the headquarters for three battalions that included my highly motivated battle buddy. Training was conducted in cycles of six weeks, allowing units to complete field exercises using air assault operations and military movement. Each iteration developed readiness for deployment cycles, times when units could be sent on short notice.

Connected to the office and our shared mission, I felt fortunate to have a strong executive officer (XO), a lieutenant colonel, as a boss detailing the requirements for my role as the Brigade Signal Officer. We had new radio systems requiring extensive training for units to communicate across greater distance with digital systems. Computer networks were tied together by radio and sometimes long stretches of wire. It was a demanding role that drew from each previous assignment and the good work of non-commissioned officers that I compared to Miller and Burke.

On Christmas Eve, the XO called me at home and told me to come to the office. His voice was flat, but I was familiar with his humor and laughed as I wished him Merry Christmas. "See you in twenty minutes."

Operation Safe Haven's purpose was to relieve the overcrowded migrant camps at Guantanamo Naval Base by establishing four camps on Empire Range, Panama. More than ten thousand Cuban migrants were moved there from Florida where they had intended to stay in the United States. As a temporary place to house them, the migrants lived in tent cities in the vicinity of Howard Air Force Base. When the decision was made that they must return to Cuba, riots broke out and military units guarding the facility were attacked.

Arriving on New Year's Eve, we set up an operations center and provided increased security for the migrants and installation. The nearby air base was used as a transportation hub for the Cuban refugees who were bussed to load planes and delivered to Guantanamo Bay. It was the trip they never expected but satisfied the decision made by the U.S. and enabled by military capabilities.

Calling back to my wife required connection via satellite that created seconds of delay. She was pregnant with our second child, a daughter, and welcomed a distant voice and update. The call had background noise and echoes that caused a delay after one stopped speaking. We learned to end sentences with "over" to let the other know it was their turn to talk. Her tolerance for erratic connections on phones was refreshed from Desert Storm and numerous leaves of absence where I called from another location. Sometimes difficult to understand, it was still affirming to hear her voice and try to weave a conversation. She talked about the due date and tried to calculate when I might return and if I could be there for the delivery.

My decision to leave active duty had evolved in previous months. The options in the private sector were numerous, and I wanted to prioritize time with my two-year-old son and coming daughter. Deliberating over the many joys I had in uniform, I considered what the next chapter might bring and told the XO that everyone had to eventually leave the boots. His caring demeanor and frequent humor made leaving more difficult but appreciated. I learned to take a step into an abyss and simply look ahead, unencumbered by not knowing exactly where I would land. Instead, I centered on the purpose and passion to get it done. Three One taught me that.

CHAPTER 11

How It Splits

WAKING EARLY AGAIN, I PULLED myself from bed and saw my phone at a glance, showing before sunrise. With jeans in hand, I headed downstairs and pushed the brew button for coffee that would be needed to provide some heat and spark to go outside. Heading out the back door, the dog dashed out before me, grateful for a chance to run and ambitious for the adventure ahead. A small wood pile at the back of our yard became a project I used for mornings, and especially mornings when I woke up in a panic.

Our small home had a basement where we placed a used wood stove that was iron and reliable. Starting a fire for heat many times in October meant there could be five months where wood was used as a primary source of heat. That requirement became a challenge I accepted, one that comprised a number of steps. The wood was delivered as logs that were not fit for pulping or milling into usable lumber. They were hardwoods taken from the nearby national forest by men who used their grit and equipment to harvest from the land. Logs varied in size but came in one truckload delivered. The best firewood contained little moisture, and the logs delivered in the spring would season over the summer as the logs were blocked and piled before they were split.

Frequently seeing the pile of wood as I pulled into our driveway daily was a way to understand where we were in the process of heating our home. Did we have logs? Were they blocked into pieces? Was there a pile of wood already split? Was there a stack of wood moved to a dry space next to the basement? Each of these were indicators for the enduring project of heating our home, one effort that contained subordinate tasks and requirements. It was equally a way to take stock of progress and appreciate that the wood provided warmth, a fundamental need, to our home. For me, the wood pile and process of splitting logs became a metaphor for my life.

The first lesson I received on splitting wood was to advantage the placement of the maul and where it hit the log. My father-in-law's insights on the most fundamental things always rang true. He saw me attempting to power through each swing and smiled as I wore myself out in minutes when I had expended every effort swinging the eight-pound mallet overhead and into the block of wood. It was simpler than that. Each piece of wood had evidence of its growth in rings, concentric circles that varied in color and complexity. Looking closely at the rings, he suggested, you could see where nature had created a fault, a hairline split offering the easiest path to maximizing the effect of eight pounds to break the log. Because he saw that line, he was in no race to try to overpower the log and make it split. He knew the route.

Focusing on where the maul hit with any precision was a simple concept, and yet controlling it required a higher level of thought. It was easier to heave the maul like a sword, but it was more effective when it hit an actual target location. This lesson taught me to see each piece of wood in some detail, looking closely enough to see any split or divide that would ease the effort required. Seeing the veins was more important than the muscle. Even knowing this truth made missing the target a little more frustrating.

In the first spring that I knew my father-in-law, he took me on a long ride to the nearby Blue Ridge Mountains. We were hunting morel mushrooms. A beautiful drive in his old Dodge truck led us to a gravel parking spot at the bottom of a steep hill leading into the dense national forest. The morning chat that filled the truck cab for our early morning departure was over. He gently set down the small foam coffee cup that he used to spit tobacco juice on the dashboard. The ham biscuit that was poorly wrapped and delicious was gone, the wrapper thrown to the floor to mix with crinkled Red Man foil packs and dirt. Brushing the crumbs decorating my shirt, I paused to look up at what lay ahead. The easy part, the portion of the trip that did not require effort, was over for now, a milestone I would admire more greatly as we exited the truck and his footsteps launched into the woodline.

Growing up near the South River and intersection of the Blue Ridge and Appalachian Mountains, my father-in-law, Roosevelt, had wisdom earned by his grit and modest upbringing. In a family of thirteen children, everyone was a gardener, everyone got up with the sun, and everyone was put to work with the lessons earned by this meager existence. Easy did not have a place to rest in their small house where at least four slept in every bedroom. Guests were perpetually welcome. He walked to and from the schoolhouse. In fact, he left early with his brothers because they had bartered their lunch meal in exchange for their sunrise arrival to start the woodstove. Roosevelt learned to split wood at an early age. The skill warmed him for decades.

Looking ahead, I saw his image escape behind trees and quickly closed the truck door to catch up. Rocks and moist leaves made steps uncertain, particularly at the pace he kept headed uphill. He moved without stopping to an elevation above 2,500 feet. It was an Olympic effort that he easily made in less than twenty minutes. I followed and grew out of breath while inhaling the fresh, cold spring air, a jolt of reality and pleasantness that blended on the side of the steep incline.

Unzipping my jacket, I felt the warmth through my shirt and sweat formed under my cap. The sunlight grew brighter as he appeared to reach the peak, a near-blinding light that I hoped would cause him to pause. Weaving through trees and branches that moved as we passed, I quickened my pace hoping to arrive alongside this sturdy man whose years were obfuscated by his athletic demonstration in mountain climbing. He felt no competition in the matter. In fact, his ambition to begin mushroom hunting was the sole catalyst for his speedy ascent. It was that simple.

Standing next to Roosevelt and huffing from the quick climb to the peak, he began a soft commentary on where we were. One leg was up on a fallen log, his right hand on the nearby tree. "You ever see a yellow poplar?" and so the teaching began about one of the places for spores and fungi that grew with moisture from downed and rotting trees. I struggled to digest the information, still recovering from the jaunt up the hill, but studied the leaves Roosevelt pointed to. They were clues for identifying trees that could point to prime morel mushroom locations.

Fortunately, the pace for mushroom hunting slowed considerably as we moved from the crested vantage point and first peak. Sun shone through trees and we studied the ground looking for these small mushrooms, a rare treat and favorite find in Rockbridge County, Virginia. My eyes roamed in search of the right leaves and to the ground where these elusive treasures could be found. Grape vines that roamed the first floor and weaved to climb trees were four inches in diameter. Layers of fallen leaves in a brilliant array of brown and orange camouflaged the mushroom's appearance and fueled the difficulty in identifying this ground layer and the honeycomb appearance of the morel.

We moved through the woods, each at a distance apart, allowing me to scan for the right tree and the right setting for this mysterious growth. Roosevelt moved incrementally, pausing when he identified a place of interest and then carefully searching for morels. His effort and leadership took us deeper and higher into the national forest, a journey he took without consideration of where he was or where to go next. His footsteps retraced routes he learned earlier with years of experience in hunting morels. As a novice to the experience, I understood I would be lost without his example and guidance.

"Ahhh," he reported, as he bent to harvest the morel from its resting place in the shadow of tall trees and wet leaves. He pulled at the base of the stem, releasing it from its foundation and with a subtle joy that provided a segue way for the next lesson. He had pulled it such a way that the entire stem and head were intact, harvested completely from its breeding space. "See here," he began, as he pointed downhill to the ground adjacent to the stand of yellow poplar. His meaty and experienced hands drew an oval in the air to explain his theory of how the morel used the fuel from the shadow and moisture to grow. The elliptical hand motion defined the likely ground for others. And just as his sentence was completed, another mushroom was obvious in the pattern he described below the tree. This morel varied in color with a brown base and grayer ridged top that was lighter at its peak.

His smile and glance to the forest ground demonstrated this life skill and admiration for how nature tied together the pieces we barely understood. I marveled at the finding, this tiny fungus, so well hidden in the leaves, that would be bypassed by others without his wisdom and fine tuning.

In a gesture I received as a tremendous privilege, Roosevelt told me to kneel and pick the next one. Taking the plastic grocery bag from my back pocket, I followed his instruction, slowly pulling at the base of the morel until its release from the moss and forest floor. "Now," he continued, "look straight ahead." Using my perspective nearer to the ground, I scanned for cousins to his first find. There were three.

In the cold morning in the backyard, the air stung my skin and made more clear a desire for heat. With a toboggan covering my ears, I looked to the yard and my wood pile seeing the dog in pursuit of the tall grass. He had made a habit of searching for groundhogs and mice, an unending effort that seemed to give him joy. Bounding through the weeds, his head moved close to the ground, his paws scratched and dug with each discovery. With a whistle, he learned to return to me, out of breath, with a wagging tail and resistance when I told him to lie down. His nose was sparked by the wood pile and movement of logs that might unveil a mouse or other smell that became his focus. My chore was to split wood for winter. His derivative chore was to identify creatures and pursue, with no frustration that he rarely bit into meat. There was no end to his commitment to search for creatures in the field, but after a few iterations of my recall, he would settle near the pile. With his tongue dangling from his mouth, he recovered slowly with a look of satisfaction on his face. His pursuit, albeit with few tangible results measured in dead animals, was his joy.

Even before sunrise, there was illumination from the moon that allowed me to study the contrast in the wood. Each log could be placed on a massive block of oak stump cut for its purpose as a flat and level base to split wood. Having each piece needing to be split, the elevation of the base placed it at the critical point of force for the swing of the maul. Turning it from side to side, I could inspect the top, looking for the circles, splits, and gaps where a well-placed maul could be effective. Each stroke was a test of my father-in-law's simple maxim. It proved its truth at every fell of the handle.

In the coldest of days, there was frost on the ground, and the wood was frozen. With remnants of moisture in the oak and hickory, winter temperatures could be an advantage for splitting wood. The wood broke more cleanly below freezing. Ice was not visible in the wood, but the force of the maul pushed apart invisible crystals and solid formations. In the winter, the wood was less soft, making the blunt force of the maul more capable of breaking it apart. This truth seemed to slightly mitigate the shocking impact of the cold wind hitting my face when I went out the back door in the darkness. Yes, it was twenty-some degrees and freezing. But for the sake of a few moments of unpleasantness until the work created warmth, the logs will be easier to split.

Seeing the circles and turning pieces to split were tips used to be effective, but the larger limitation was physical strength and stamina. Neighbors recommended the use of their gas-powered splitter, a hydraulic lever that pushed twenty-one tons of pressure to make the wood split. No question it was more efficient than my by-hand preference, save for the appreciation I had gained for the task. Yes,

I would comment, in expressing thanks for their offer, the log splitter was a better way. At least it seemed that way at a distance.

I felt fortunate for that chance to see each facet of the process from the logs being delivered to the blocks that needed to be split. I had developed an outlet for silently solving problems while fuel was split to warm our home. It was a map of sorts for the seasons and established a requirement that fed my interest in warmth, with the chance to earn the wood's heat. The log splitter created noise, a distraction for my poor hearing and chance to hear the morning field come to life with birds, cows moving to the fenceline, and the barks of the dog as he tried to herd. The exercise of splitting wood was a more simple pleasure, a task that I used to expend energy and contrast the desk job that paid the bills.

With each stroke of the maul, I stared at the small area and learned to aim eight pounds effectively with more precision. When it required more effort, I raised it higher, frequently frustrated by a knot in the log or my ineffective blow. As much as a physical contest to swing the appliance, splitting wood required a mental acuity to sustain the effort. The work fueled other thoughts and distilled problems I saw more clearly through the process of breaking wood apart. In my mind, I set up scenarios that required my strength and considered the problems I could not solve. I stacked and unstacked them, sometimes throwing ideas in a pile and seeing others as ready to burn. Where I felt anger, I poured it into the handle and saw it impact the oak. I grew tired from exploring these ideas and felt the sweat on my brow. I inhaled the fresh smell of the hardwood, an inspiration for its natural goodness and also the visual result of my swing.

Getting out to the field early meant not having any competing demand for regular work or the family still well asleep inside. It was me and the dog. And my effort to solve and stack wood. Many times, exhausted easily in under an hour, I could walk slowly back up the hill with a tired dog and some of my anxieties expended on an unwitting piece of wood. The day might bring many more problems, but I felt some gratitude for getting some points on the board before it all began.

When I graduated from a wheelbarrow to a trailer to pull behind the lawn tractor, the process of stacking wood near the house was made exponentially easier. Each of our three boys savored the chance to add machinery to the process, either by riding in my lap or by making the circuit from the log pile to the house. At every level, they disliked the stacking, and yet the effort baked cooperation into them even before the fire was lit. They shuttled wood from one to the other and stacked pieces against the house. They paced themselves and learned to throw the wood from one to another, sometimes landing on a leg and causing more complaints. Bitter as they were at times for the requirement to stack wood, in what they perceived as an unending chore, the wood stove and permission to light a fire drew fascination.

The basement of our brick home was the parking place for the woodstove that allows heat to rise to the upper floor. Cold winter and wind burned the wood to create a cycle of filling the stove twice a day to keep it burning. A special delight was to open the stove in the morning and see remaining embers still shimmering from air flow. Stepping to the back porch to get pieces to replenish the fire, the cold air rushed into the basement. Kneeling then in front of the stove, each piece could be placed on the embers. When the doors were pulled almost shut, the air rushed through the chimney and heated the embers. Sounds of air moving and the crackles of dry wood began the day with another cycle of heat, the last step in the process that brought warmth.

In what could have been a three-car garage to our home, Roosevelt had developed a barbershop in a partitioned space with a separate door. The old chair that filled its center was the one his father, also a trained barber, used for the years he had the barbershop in the small town outside of the South River. When Roosevelt returned from Korea, he used his GI Bill to pay tuition for his training, giving him a living and way to work alongside his favorite person. Together, they stood next to men and listened with their ears while trimming the hair around the others.

Barbering required craft on a number of levels. There was the artform of matching lines to conform to a person's head. A good haircut was made premium when the barber studied the head and patterns of hair growth for its natural angle and direction. Simply cutting it was not enough. Hair combed naturally from one side to another, many times with small cowlicks and changes that were different with each person. Roosevelt knew that detail. He also understood more deeply that while he was cutting hair, he served another person. It was not that hair covered one's ears but rather that each one needed to be heard. That was a real barber.

Trimming hair required movement of the head, an element Roosevelt managed firmly in his grip. Hands that milked cows, split wood, and pulled a plow through a garden were strong and gritty. When it was time to taper the haircut from the base on the neck, his large palm covered the head and gently moved it for his shears. Sometimes the hand would linger, holding a head like a cantaloupe being inspected before purchase. He tilted, pressed, and moved it as needed so that he could maneuver around the barber chair and reach every angle.

In absorbing the words and issues for each customer, "Rosie," a nickname assigned by his customers, the barber became a local favorite and someone to trust. A man of few words, he digested the conversation of the shop carefully, only commenting when needed. As a result of his conservation and allergy to simple chatter, he offered deeper replies and asked insightful questions. For those who wanted better grooming, they could pause in the shop and gain commentary from other patrons sprinkled with pithy phrases from Rosie, a treat almost as valuable as the precise trim of his clippers.

The small building next to his garage became a woodshed and his storage for racks of split wood used for Roosevelt's wood stove. In seasons when my pile was stacked, I was able to assist in getting his stock organized and bring dry pieces to his porch for use. The exchange remained lopsided with his years dedicated to the task and my limited contribution to his woodshed space.

On a winter evening, I pulled into his driveway, my youngest in tow, and saw Roosevelt leaning into a deer hung by its back legs as he carved the meat. His pocket knife, the same sharp instrument he carried for years, moved from the inside of the skin, peeling it in his effort to carve the deer into pieces that could be frozen. The boy quickly arrived at his side with a barrage of questions and curiosity for the dead animal and his grandfather standing next to it upside down. He answered the first few but was working actively to move the knife and complete his task.

The cold air of the evening had not distracted the butcher; he was keenly focused on the small knife. As I moved closer to him, I saw his grip on the deer leg more firmly and noticed that he was using that for stability. He carved lower into the animal and then stood up completely when the aroma of alcohol made me understand his unstable position and disregard for the cold. Fear swelled inside me. He began the story of how a friend had shared the meat with him knowing that he would enjoy the venison. Somewhere in the exchange they enjoyed fellowship with some drinking. I interrupted to comment about my little one needing the bathroom and dismissed him to wander inside the home, away from the cold and this lingering moment.

I stepped back from the shed and considered my own pattern of drinking and then making a decision to stop. This was a commitment I made to myself dozens of times in more than two decades, each time with a little more regret than the last. I was missing the mark in many ways, reminiscent of the logs and my varying aim at the circles and fissures of the wood. My critical eye of him standing next to the poorly butchered animal was a look inside my own struggle to be upright. I had the facts and experience of my own father, and I had regrets that his death at fifty-four had not been more of a sober catalyst for changing my own actions. With the swing of the maul, I thought of how I measured up to be effective in other areas. I was losing.

In times when we drove together in his truck, Roosevelt provided a variety of topics for our discussion. Although his school completion was measured only by the fifth grade, his wisdom endured and was centered on foundational principles. He was never shy to use the Bible as a primary way to know what was right, weaving together the rich fabric of his modest upbringing. I considered him one of the wisest men I know.

Seeing him in the woodshed, I saw the pattern of my own bouts with drinking and the way it influenced my footsteps. Knowing the recurring pattern plagued me, I wrestled with being abstinent and recognizing the propensity for alcoholism that I inherited. With a stomach cancer diagnosis the previous year, Roosevelt endured the complex surgery to remove it and allow the body to create a new storage space for nutrition. After months of tube feeding and patience, he gained strength that offered him another chapter and renewed interest in his passions. He visited an old cabin, a hunting camp he built with his brothers, near the Blue Ridge Parkway where there was a pond and plenty of walking space. He gained strength to slowly climb again to the high spots where the morels grew and sparked his memory. He settled at times to retell stories and gave others a chance to listen.

The days in the barbershop were fewer after the cancer. He scaled back to one day per week but still enjoyed those returning allies and the familiar exchange of local news and tales from the past. He drove the old roads of the parkway that he knew well, reliving his experience as a young man and savoring days when he was strong enough to step outside.

Late in the summer, I shared an evening watching baseball with Roosevelt. He was quieter now, resigning to his failing health and the return of cancer that took its toll in other areas. He offered no comment on the pitching. He did not move from his chair to the kitchen to sneak something to eat. He did not engage in the questions of the day or invest much in response to my inquiries. He was comfortable in the chair watching his Braves, a decades-long pattern of evening pastime and pleasure.

Slowly turning to me, he offered me directions to go to his gun cabinet. "Pick out one of those guns," and seeing my uncertain frown, he added, "I want you to have one." I moved to the cabinet and picked up the 12-gauge shotgun that had been with us for rabbit hunting. I came back to the couch and told him why this gun was special to me, feedback he almost received but did not fully take in. I expressed my deepest thanks, with tears, knowing it was a parting gift, but saw his face was blank. His energy and emotions were receding, giving way to his disease and what he knew was his eventual departure. In what he could control over remaining days, he parsed out items intended to share and gave the humble direction of what he expected next.

Awkwardly holding the shotgun next to the couch where he was without emotion, I recounted the days when he introduced me to hunting rabbits. I remembered following him to the shed where he kept beagles who were critical to the fall endeavor. They barked and yipped as he put them in the small kennel on the truck bed before we drove to nearby neighbors and old farm places. Letting the dogs loose, we saw them scamper to nearby bushes with their nose tightly pinned to the grass and any hints of smell. The dogs roamed in a group and used their own barking to alert the others that a rabbit was nearby, a signal that ignited the group in a burst of barking before they launched onto a trail.

In my initial days of rabbit hunting, the dogs were an amazing sight, and I hustled to keep up with their irregular path. In large shrubs or bushes, the beagles wrestled their way inside the low branches, lightly barking to broadcast their position. Rabbits that had dashed for the cover of the briar bush were scared from the resting spot and brought into the open for the hunter. Moving quickly behind them, I marveled at the effort of these dogs and their instinctive appetite for chase.

The beagles scampered up the hill and changed direction too many times to be followed, a challenge I accepted before losing to their ability to quickly move from sight. It was in the absence of seeing the beagles that Roosevelt revered most, slightly tilting his head to wait for the wind or an echo from his animals still in pursuit. I learned to stand near him, frustrated by not keeping pace with the dogs and feeling responsible for them vanishing into the woodline. With a wry smile, he unleashed another grand lesson, justifying his calm and unconcerned stance. He explained his few footsteps and recounted his love for the dogs doing their work and signaling the hunt for rabbits. But he understood the nature of the rabbit as well, who would run from their den to evade the beagle but, once tired from running, would eventually return. Roosevelt knew this formula and instinctive reality, a simple truth that bloomed a number of lessons. Many things come around to where they begin if you are patient to let it happen. At a distance from the furry feet we hunted together, I thought of my own footsteps chasing in one direction when the truth was typically not running away. It was a test of patience and an ability to understand problems more completely. Remember and learn where a pattern starts, and be willing to solve it from the beginning.

Staring again at the aligned log placed on a firmer stump to be split, I remembered the few words he shared instructing me to see the lines and natural faults. Two sentences of data on the frailty of the wood translated to piles of fuel for heat. I wished I had absorbed the lessons more completely and not been so biased to my own effort to simply whack the wood with a heavy maul before placing it with intent. I had learned enough to repeat the task and become more efficient. I had benefited from stacking the wood with insights gained in breaking it into pieces. I treasured the morning fire, rekindled with dry pieces for fuel. I discovered the limits of my own ability and was reminded with every swing. I considered the stack of my problems remaining and knew the quiet deliberation of the morning helped me distill truths. I had seen inside the way the logs were made, and began to understand it was the maker, the author of the tall oak and knotty hickory, that provided ways to create heat and ingest meaning from the work.

CHAPTER 12

Work, Drink & Cancer

FRIENDS WHO SHARED THEIR COLONOSCOPY testimony were correct, the preparation was much more elaborate than the procedure. Laying in the hospital bed, the attendant appeared at my feet to wrap a warm blanket to cover my torso. On a day when I anticipated other probing, the experience began with luxurious treatment that seemed more like a spa.

Awakening in a recovery room, the attendant was kind enough to bring a hot cup of coffee to me as I returned. The doctor, a family friend from church, was cordial and quick in delivering good news that the procedure showed no evidence of problems. In fact, he suggested another colonoscopy could wait another ten years. I felt relief in the news, not because I expected problems, but because his narrative was positive and clear. Checkbox for the wellness task completed when I turned fifty.

I approached the fifth decade with a perspective biased by the early death of both parents and my brother. We are all prone to consider our prospects for living, and both of the men in my life passed before either turned fifty-five. I had quit smoking many years ago, but as I considered aging, I thought of the changes I should have made many years before. Many years.

I was recruited into a Fortune 500 management trainee program for junior military officers when I left the Army as a captain. They were interested in the communications and electronics experience that the military had provided. It was a technology enterprise, and they sought the maturity needed to build leaders in the organization. We relocated to a small town in Kentucky where a number of manufacturing companies had planted roots for offices and large distribution centers.

I let my hair grow after almost fifteen years, maintaining a tapered cut and grooming requirements. Longer hair seemed unnatural to me, perhaps more by the ample evidence of my balding than by the lack of practice in letting the hair touch my ears. I tried to look the part of a civilian.

The New Yorker magazine was my account. Each week, they sent artwork, pictures, and paper copy that was typeset for printing. The presses at our location printed paged sections, advertising, and cards that could be added to make different versions of the magazine. Instructions for the magazine pages and composition were written in AS400, a computer assembly language designed to operate on mainframe computers connected to the printing floor. More than 800,000 copies were printed each week, with special detail paid to select almost 300 that were perfect.

For the World Economic Forum held annually in Davos, Switzerland, freshly printed magazines were needed to place with key political figures and influencers. As one of few that had a valid passport, the trip to Europe was part of my duties. As a courier, I carried the newest copies of the New Yorker magazine to their publisher, flying first to Stockholm and then moving by train to the forum venue.

A quick trip to another continent might have been a benefit, save for the wait between stops and the shift in time zones. It was not a vacation. On the evening of the third day, I finally handed over the prized box of office copies to a smiling face who dashed to the door to greet notable figures who would receive their copy. Duties completed, I checked into the hotel and made my way to their dining room.

The first beer was recommended by the waiter, one of the sons of the family-run lodging. It was a wheat beer, a reminder of tastes I enjoyed in Germany, a hearty and natural flavor that seemed to have more weight. I felt mildly obligated by the suggestion, but after half the glass, I knew it was more than thirst that attracted me to the beverage. After enjoying a platter of noodles and savory beef, the second beer brought a buzz and dull feeling that accelerated my sleepiness.

Waking before sunrise to catch the return train to Stockholm, I had a few minutes to brush my teeth but not enough time to rid myself of the headache. I felt regret. One beer would have been enough. Perhaps dehydrated, my mouth felt dry and my stomach tense with angst in indulging again. The slope was everything and slippery.

In the second job after separating from the Army, I was cast to carry a message and met with groups to give presentations. We relocated to Virginia, and I had a sense that the job more naturally met my passions and experience. Even so, traveling for work and the emotional cost of a speaking part were an odd pairing. The military had well trained me for reporting and briefing audiences on a variety of topics. But I was an introvert placed into an extrovert position. I was still not trained on keeping myself in check. That required footsteps that matched the voice track.

Traveling to different locations added variety to the work and diluted the time I could be with family. In the transition, we absorbed the adjustment to lower pay than the corporate world, but I was hopeful the rewards and future would even the numbers. It was a good thought, but perhaps not realistic with a family. After months of conversation, I was persuaded to join the Army National Guard and was assigned to a unit that had lineage to D-Day. The lexicon of reserve component service was vastly different, although the fabric, the people, and the processes were more than familiar. A new circle of comrades and business were woven together in ways I had not expected. At the same time, the new secondary role was distinct and separate with another outfit and identity miles from home.

A friend warned me about swear words, the profanity that litters our language. His caution was that much like an iceberg, the words that rose above the surface to be heard emanated from a place covered in foul language. This indictment proved true as I first met people in the infantry unit. I joined their vernacular easily and, in retrospect, marvel at how quickly my thoughts included the same descriptions and words. I saw how easily I walked away from a desire to communicate well and not succumb to the simple cussing. It wasn't the legalism of it, but rather the truth that, for me, bad language infected my thoughts. I was less kind and considerate as a result of the words that went from thought to spoken word. Part of my disappointment was my own appraisal that I was a chameleon, adapting to my environment and falling prey to a need to be accepted. It is not who I wanted to be.

Returning from a trip to California, my sister called to tell me my brother had died. He was fifty-two and tending to the Christmas lights in his front yard when he expired. My hero, taken too young. Flying from Virginia, I was exhausted after a restless night thinking of the loss of my idol. Seven years of age difference was never an obstacle for our alignment, his uneven and intermittent communication always finished my last sentence. With my head leaned forward in the seat, I awoke at intervals and burst into tears. My oldest put his hand on my arm and, once awakened, I saw my lapse drawing the attention of other passengers.

I had visited Joe in the fall prior to his death. He was recovering from cardiac problems he inherited that persisted with smoking. We had a conversation about cigarettes, drinking, and our genetics. His warnings were genuine and made more credible by his history and the shadow of our parent's death. Absent a decision to guide ourselves away from these risks, the destination was more clear.

Walking from his funeral marker to the opposing hill where my parents were laid to rest, I missed them deeply and knew their lives were cut short. I was reminded of the cigarettes I continued to smoke after Dad's heart surgery. My pattern with drinking was the same.

I was missing the message, ignoring it while the evidence continued to surround me. The pillars of my connection to people were leaving, and for reasons that should have led me to change.

Travel and some weekend military duty soon became a full schedule with a growing number of trips and distances. Oddly, the schedule and audience created more opportunity for escape, first to another night away from responsibilities at home, and then the added layer of darkness that gave me room to indulge. A suit and tie to portray the corporate character, and then pulling a camouflage uniform from the trunk for the next days of military duty.

Not wanting to be a boozer, I opted for cream sherry, a sweet port wine, as a preferred drink. I bought it at grocery stores after evening meetings. I bought it on the way to weekend reserve duty obligations. The effects took hold quickly, reminding me of the invitation to enjoy a buzz more than my reality.

In long drives and in moments of reflection, I took stock of how drinking poured into me just as the words. I wished some of it were different, but I saw the facade with clarity. A proper dad at home with great kids, a uniform to wear, a spokesman role at work, and the accouterments of a pleasant life. I felt the distance between my footsteps, saying one thing and doing another. Day after day, I sought solace that I was not being taken over by a behavior or substance but was left with only the cold comfort that I endured another day and still mostly looked the part.

Sorting problems on a log to split was an outlet for energy. Swinging a maul allowed success when the log split fairly. And frustration when the knots got in the way. It was in these morning sessions that I thought about how I was headed in the wrong direction. The headache and the reddening face should have alerted me. Even slow rain eventually makes you soaked. I had no umbrella or shield for the pattern and strong desire to drink. For me, the wine was not a beverage but more of a destination.

Drinking alone in a hotel room, it was easy to settle in for some mindless video and pour glasses of wine into the dark. I planned a phone call home before the booze made me different. If my speech slurred, I bragged about being tired. I knew I was hiding.

I had been to a variety of men's Bible studies where a testimony of recovering from drinking was celebrated. It was easy to cheer the admission and certainly the victory. I listened intently, wondering if one day it would be me. Would I ever get to the other side of this? I never heard the testimony or prayer request for porn. No one prayed that they be spared a connection to this muddy water. No one described the faucet of pornography that was so easy to turn on and so effective in drawing us to our lust without ever quenching our thirst. I wondered why I never heard the words with these admissions, and then I was deafened by my own collusion to the substance and unwillingness to pray for forgiveness. The dim light of a small room in many towns is where the shadow of pornography pulled me down. Sadly, the internet optimized its capacity to infect simply by its scale and the algorithm that so readily suggested the next thing to see, somehow related, and soon landing us in places we would never admit we liked.

I thought so many times of not wanting to fail this way. But it was so easy. Being drunk slowly eroded a commitment to turn over a new leaf.

Alcohol does a better job of dehydrating. Soon after the second glass poured, trips to the bathroom increased. Often, I looked to the mirror entering the bathroom, seeing my tilted gait and visible changes to my eyes. My nose was red, partly from rosacea fed by drinking that created varicose veins over time. I looked the part. I saw it every time I looked in the mirror.

Many times, waking to an early alarm, I found myself collapsed on a chair or laid across the bed, never taking cover in the sheets. Passing out had become a routine.

In the years of travel, I saw the pattern more clearly, making continual promises that I would change. I prayed it would be different. For board meetings when I reported to officers, I worked diligently to prepare presentations but made a calendar mark for the day I would stop drinking. In the beginning, ten or more days of abstinence allowed the red face to subside. Twenty-one days was the longest I made it. The calendar was decorated with broken promises, each one creating regret and adding to my rhyming narrative. I had a problem that was getting worse in physical ways, but the deficits to the body easily translated to anxiety in the morning.

After a long Saturday of weekend military duty, I reserved a room at the back end of the small military post. Unfancy rooms were perfect, cheap, and available in short order. I stopped at the store to get salad, intending to be healthy, but also got the larger bottle of sherry. Soon, the warmth of those gulps translated to uneven steps and trips to the bathroom.

The first time I talked to myself in the mirror, I knew it was abnormal. Reminded of my father's axiom, I knew we all had to look ourselves in the mirror. His comment stuck with me, "Never cut yourself shaving." With that caution, he meant that men are accountable and should be able to face themselves, an admonition to do things well and be upright. My face appearing in the mirror fueled my self-criticism and outbursts of anger. I yelled like I was the toughest kid on the playground looking for a fight. I yelled at the little boy who was doing it wrong. I frequently repeated, "Who do you think you are?" I contorted my face with the question. And then said it again, then internalizing the conflict of this other person who I became when I was away and with the bottle. It wasn't long before I imagined I saw the little boy too weak and afraid to tell someone or make it stop.

On a raining dark morning, I pulled on my uniform and went to the bathroom, seeing the broken mirror and chards of glass in the sink. Puzzled, I stared into the remnant of shining glass that remained. I saw part of my face before lowering my eyes to see the cuts on my knuckles.

It was Father's Day when my younger son, Joseph, wrote an intentional letter to express his gratitude. He was a reader at four, a compounding learning effect absorbed by observing the pattern of two older siblings with homeschooling. His letters were straight, and

I marveled at how such a young boy would write such a long letter. At seven, he had carefully crafted the lines for two pages and called me the "wood chopper," something he admired with details of how he saw hard work. I was heartened by his observation and analogy but equally struck by the distance between the upright man he thought he saw and the person I became when I was away. The maul hit my ego in the seam between these two characters.

I was a clanging bell in selling the colonoscopy appointment for my lovely wife, Terry. She was far more healthy and balanced the demands of being a mother, working as a nurse, with a lifelong commitment to her health. Her modest discontent for the doctor appointment was based on time: the time it took away from a busy schedule and the hours required for preparation. As a nurse, she easily recognized the merit of the procedure, but fitting it into a complex calendar was a challenge.

As an ambassador for the procedure, it was natural to guide her to the appointment and to support her in this milestone. As it turned out, she did not favor the warm blanket as I had. She was more oriented on completion and returning to the pace and duties she paused to make this out-patient procedure.

John was kind enough to let me sit in his office when she was wheeled away, allowing me a moment to be grateful for his friendship and special care for my bride. When he returned, his face was all business while I thanked him for the respite of his office and time to care for her. After sitting, his face remained still before telling me. "Yes," he started, "the procedure identified no problems in her colon." He then looked at me more intently to explain how he took a biopsy of an external area that he thought was cancer.

The warmth of his small office went away. Blood rushed to my face and sweat formed on my head. I had no response and only thought of this lightning bolt of news: my best friend may have cancer.

When the results came back six days later, I was prepared for the worst news, and yet Dr. John shared a more positive report. The tissue was not cancerous. In fact, he scheduled a surgery to remove the affected skin simply as a measure of caution and to preclude any chance of cancer growth. Crisis averted, I pivoted to accompany her to the University of Virginia where an experienced colleague would surgically remove the problem area.

My daughter sat with me at the University of Virginia Medical Center. In a large foyer, a medical student placed their backpack next to the stool and leaned into the piano keys. People talked softly as they moved through the area. Smells of coffee added comfort to this well-established place where uncertainty persisted. The notes echoed through a tall ceiling and provided a lift and some moments of contemplation as we held hands and prayed for a successful surgery. This should be simple. He was an expert. John said he was the best. Terry never feared the word like I did. She was always much taller.

My phone rang and a calm voice detailed why they had not proceeded. An examination and surgical review identified cancer. That was not simple.

Soft piano music and pleasant surroundings did not stop my tears. Sobbing into my daughter's shoulder, I felt disbelief more than sadness. This couldn't be true. It was. The expert just told me.

Her hand held my shoulder, and Anna looked at me without the tears that covered me. "The God that we prayed to, the one who we believed would make this okay, He is the same God that loves Mom and will protect her." At the moment, I would have been happier if she had joined my sorrow. But I had to contend with the one God, indeed, the same source of hope in any circumstance. I looked away and tried to reconcile what she had said. The evidence of her mother's faith beamed through her even when the sun was not shining.

With support from friends, the schedule of appointments was shared, and the winding road of treatment began. Radiation was a trip into a dystopian future seeing the love of my life lifted into a huge machine with lasers pointing to marked spots on her pelvis. Holding her hand before the machine began its clanking, she pulled up the blanket and could easily return my stare with a quick smile. Wearing my lead-filled vest, I walked through the thick vault door to stand outside to a small observer's window and saw my bride close her eyes before the table moved forward and the rattling of the radiation apparatus began the forty-minute cycle.

Terry does not fear death. She fears not living, truly being alive, every day that she has on Earth. She was tired after treatments but, oddly, wanted to ensure we stopped afterward so I could eat or we could sit together. She never said it hurt.

Friends were quick to provide support and took turns in the morning trips to the cancer center. With flexibility in a work schedule, I tried to prioritize these days and could dedicate the morning to the shuttle and return. Warm baths were a way to treat drying skin and associated pain from the affected area. Before loading my laptop into the car, I put on a tie and tried to set her up for rest when I left for work. I made some tea, she thanked me for the bath and insisted she would get in shortly.

I was opening the car door before I realized my briefcase was still inside the house. I had set it down before the tea and missed it hurrying to get back to the office. Stepping into the kitchen, I easily spotted the case and reached for it when her screams rang through the house. She cried and yelled about the excruciating pain that covered her when she lowered her body into the hot bath. Her wailing fueled my hurried ascent up the stairs to try and rescue her, but when I got to the door, her sobbing stopped. She never wanted me to see that part.

Startled from my pattern and episodic sobriety, I made a rigid promise to myself to be free of alcohol and the regret that had tormented me for decades. I was sober. I had to be.

I left months later for Maryland when my National Guard unit was called to active duty in support of Operation Enduring Freedom. It was the second call-up in my reserve service and a far more complex involuntary set of orders for four hundred days. I would command soldiers from seven states called up to create a new formation, a specialized task force with high-end information technology and cybersecurity experience.

Each mobilized soldier would be required to pass the counter-intelligence polygraph, a rigorous set of certification requirements for a mission that was completely new and would remain unknown until we arrived. My top-secret clearance was up for a five-year review, checking all changes since the last investigation and in-person interviews with my named and related references. In what was intended as a sidebar comment, one of my field grade officers joked that he would carefully answer questions when he was interviewed for my case. In the questions relating to my behavior and any use of drugs or alcohol, there was inquiry about mental fitness. "It's not an evening of fellowship with you as much as it is blood sport," a comment with accuracy that stung to my core. Was I going to lose my clearance if they learned more, dug for details, or asked more questions?

One hundred days was little preparation time for a deployment of this sort where questions outpaced understanding. We formed a small team that traveled to unit locations to share what we could and marveled at the level of talent brought into this space. Soldiers whose civilian occupation was also critical to their business had the difficult conversation of leaving soon, often without someone to backfill their sought-after skills. In my own sphere, I had a similar conversation, awkward in not sharing many details and not having a barometer for their genuine level of support. It's easy to say we support your service as a business, but more than fifteen years into recurring deployments, the practical application varied greatly.

I departed days early for Maryland where most of the mission could be conducted and relied on an efficient pick-up team of talented technicians. Together, we set the stage for Task Force Echo, the largest call-up of cyber forces in the history of the Department of Defense (DOD). One hundred and fifty people left their life behind to be a part of operations they could never talk about. Our mission was to secure and defend critical infrastructure, computer networks and systems, that were essential to operations for the newly formed United States Cyber Command.

The demands of a three-star headquarters were far more complex and required deep dives into new processes, intelligence, and mission requirements. New in both form and function, Task Force Echo navigated the winding road to apply soldiers to synchronize with operations in a battlespace that was continents away. Trips to the Pentagon and recurring briefings to senior leaders became part of the initial cadence and new schedule.

Back in an apartment adjacent to a mall, I was a short commute to work conveniently subject to recall and working extended hours. With my sobriety intact, I built defenses, internalizing how vulnerable I felt away from the foundations of home and my ordinary life. Absent the sedation that drinking seemed to provide, the distance from me and my internal struggles seemed more present and palpable. The long narrative continued. No place to hide, and with new light shining on the guy who tried to keep the reputation and appearance unsoiled.

I changed my schedule for an earlier rise and hit the elliptical machine to sweat before the day began. It was better to be tired than comfortable and head down the slope so familiar to me. By now, I had more than five hundred days without drinking, and I counted each one.

Stress played an active part in stirring me to block old habits, but the angst was increased substantially with responsibility for this hybrid mission with ample visibility. Headaches came back with veracity, and I saw my energy as the limited resource drawn to work demands as well as my life in the background. Waking early, I fell into a routine of coffee that should have been one cup but grew longer when thoughts ruminate and lead me to darkness.

Trying to piece together a routine, my sleep was plagued with nightmares of a black wolf attacking me through a cloud of smoke. Outside the Ramaila oil fields, set afire by exiting Iraqi troops in Desert Storm, the wind blew smoke thick enough to create dense and surreal darkness in the daylight hours. The beast's low growl was aimed at me in furious anger. I was startled awake and felt the pit of shame take hold. Laying on the couch and unable to return to sleep, I scrolled through videos that started with news but were soon filled with clips of Arlington Cemetery. Migraines made darkness feel like safety. Movement blurred my ability to focus and made me nauseous.

Why was the reality of an amazing mission so overshadowed with my own internal narrative doubting the sanctity of my facade? What happens if the questions, interviews, and clearance investigation unveil instances where my behavior fell short? Why am I spiraling? If I ask for help now, what will happen to this tour of duty and my continued service? How can it be that my sobriety has not removed the clouds that darkened my days?

On a rainy night, I screamed myself awake when the wolf came back breathing into my face. I pulled open the nightstand where my gun rested and moved to the window.

CHAPTER 13

Secret Requirements

WHEN I WAS "READ ON" to the programs at the National Security Agency (NSA), we swore an oath to protect the information we worked on. Nothing of the work we did could be shared. The indoctrination program included a thorough reading of the requirements for each member. This was an hours-long presentation. Affirmations of requirements were explained before we signed in ink. Once complete, we stood with a right hand raised and uttered the words indicating our agreement to not share information. I made a promise for a term that would expire in the year 2042.

Over the more than two decades of work and assignments in the specialized space of cyber operations, I have appreciated the responsibility with classified information and take it seriously. As part of the requirement, there is a particular way that transcripts like this book are to be shared and ultimately approved from the agency. I take no issue with such a high expectation and consider it a privilege that I was trusted at that level.

Even so, it is interesting to reflect on the extent to which the requirement for secrecy has been a recurring theme in my own life, apart from the requirements for the agency. Growing up in a dysfunctional home, I learned the daytime rules of getting along and could easily recognize when the alcohol changed the parents I said goodbye to that morning. After the torment of and episodic scenes with the man who abused me, I understood too well that harboring those realities was critical to my survival. I learned too late of its harm. In the days when my anxiety heightened and sparks of Post Traumatic Stress Disorder (PTSD) shook my normal, I understood the culture and context that largely expected these moments to be internalized. The sum of many of these exposures was a lesson confirming a need, in homage to someone else and at great personal cost, to not share information.

Growing up, I learned there was a time for questions and another time where disagreement should be avoided. There were things you could say out loud, and then there were topics that were off limits. There were memories of good times that brought laughter, and there were moments to be forgotten, never to be given words. There were emotions that could be felt and absorbed, and then there were parameters for how one should act. Complaints had a place not resident in our space. There were roles for parents and then specific characters and directions for the children. The stage had rules and, more importantly, obligations. This was the construct for our home. Stay inside the profile or suffer the consequences.

For that reason, a deep understanding for following the rules, I was a case study of the profile needed for a pedophile to prey upon, knowing full well the dogma would keep the perversion safe. So, the military secrecy requirement added another layer, but one where the rudiments were oddly the same. Never say a word. No need to know. We will test the veracity of your adherence to this promise.

The first time I sat for a counterintelligence polygraph, I had to travel several hours to get to the installation where the office was located. I was provided detailed instructions on precisely when to arrive and how not to prepare. Dietary suggestions included eating a modest breakfast and not relying too much on caffeine. My usual three cups would have to wait. Given that the procedure included measuring biometric data, there was a strong suggestion that there be no physical exercise or prolonged exertion. The sum of the various requirements and recommendations set a foundation for a much-increased sense of anxiety for me.

I purposefully arrived the night prior to the test and ensured it was acceptable to wear civilian clothes for the appointment. My late-night pattern would not work. I had to be well rested, even if that was in contrast with my wanting to sleep. I entered the plain building, signed into the waiting room, and considered how I had exaggerated the importance of this test. I fueled competition with myself. My mind raced about what to expect and the ingredients of this mysterious insight into my worthiness to be trusted at a higher level.

My mind was still ruminating on the concept of my merit and trust when the proctor for the test described the process. He described what would take place in what I considered boring detail, the evolution that would take place over the next ninety minutes. Bands were connected to my wrists, legs, and across my chest. I was to sit still, to answer questions, and to remain focused on the directions he would provide through questions. Once complete, he reiterated the requirement never to share details of the questions or to collude with others in order to prepare for the test. Of course, I thought, this aligned with decades of my own personal experience.

As predicted, it was ninety minutes when he indicated that we were finished and disassembled the bands and sensors. It felt like hours. That was the moment that I took stock of my shirt that was pressed in the morning and was now fully wrinkled and wet. My midsection looked like I had been wrapped in spirals, evidence of the sweat and angst that had subtly worked me over.

Affirming my oath again years later at the NSA, I reflected on that initiation into the requirements and protections of the intelligence community. The small classroom was full and each of the attendees met that same requirement. Their allegiance had also been tested and each were confirmed; these were people who would keep a secret.

Such a small sub-section of people work in this space. I felt honored to be invited, and yet equally considered my pedigree. Was I good at this because I was competent? Or was I better qualified because of the pattern of secrets and dysfunction that preceded my military service? It was an inquiry worthy of my consideration, but one that felt weighty. I took the oath with the solemnity it deserved, albeit adding to the burden already resident and internal to me.

As part of daily military operations, it would not be unusual for another entity or person to request access to projects or information from my unit. In deliberating on their access, the criteria is "need to know," a guardrail created to ensure that the right people had the right information. There was an inherent requirement not to allow those whose duties did not overlap operationally to have access to the information. As a principle, it makes every bit of sense. Share what needs to be shared. In contrast, not that one would use it this way, the elements of our own story and the problems we harbor do not always find safe harbor. For me, too many of these were quarantined in my own ruminations and internal angst. The embargo on truth caused pain.

Part of my tireless analysis of the polygraph examination was in the biometrics that are derivative of any examination. Each of the leads and wires connected to a person created a measurable output, a number that was tracked and collected. This precise data had been validated over time to substantiate where frailty exists in a person's testimony or performance of duty. Was there a measure for the wall of safekeeping I created?

My consideration was the extent to which my own experiences might also emanate from me. Was my lack of confidence and awkwardness in youth measurable just as the truth was signaled through this examination? Could people see that I was damaged goods? Was there some behavior or outward body language that let others know? Was I marked and understood this way?

I tried to silence my concerns with footsteps and focus on mission. It was another rock in my ruck sack. Duty required these obligations, and I had to compartmentalize the parts of me that were as yet unresolved. They were simply requirements vice the measure of who I truly was.

CHAPTER 14

You're A Star?

THE FIRST PHONE CALL RELATED to my future promotion to brigadier general came from a longtime friend from the Virginia Army National Guard. He was an expert in the process of being vetted and selected for promotion. He knew the extensive packet of credentials and detailed records that formed the candidate file for review. He definitely knew the most likely outcome.

"Congratulations," he began, "I have a retirement gift for you." We laughed as he explained that my nomination had been confirmed; I had a certificate of eligibility for promotion to the next higher rank after colonel. His lightheartedness was well placed. Nominees were selected and then a larger bench, a list of those offered the certificate, was created as a potential list of those who could be tapped for flag officer positions. Receiving the certificate only meant the list, and very few rose from that status position to opportunities to don the one-star rank.

His cynicism and humor were pleasant, and I appreciated both his candor and the personal touch of calling me, knowing that the senior person in the state, a two-star general, would call me soon for official notification. The first call leveled expectations. And this would be especially true for my circumstance, a colonel serving in cyber formations, a niche so small in the DOD and with an even smaller footprint in the reserve component. I was the first ever to be selected and eligible, but even further complicating the small circle was the lack of any positions to serve in. No vacancies and no pathway. A really nice retirement gift that I could smile about but that would never manifest in uniform. A silent accolade that I accepted.

Sergeant First Class Nunneley, a worn veteran of Vietnam-era service, met us at the bus arriving at Fort Rucker, Alabama, shortly after midnight. We were to get off his bus. We were moving too slow. We looked like sacks of potatoes. It was actually his Army. He would teach us where the sun rose. He was our senior drill sergeant, the first among a dozen giants that walked with us and slept with us in the days of Basic Training.

I thought of him as I reflected moments after hanging up the phone and discussion of potential promotion. At seventeen, Drill Sergeant Nunnelley's vibrant welcome was a startling moment when reality took over the recruiter's message and my expectations in joining the Army. Apparently, it was not all rainbows. Nunnelley knew so many things we did not and could not know. He vehemently disliked why we joined the Army, an obligation paired with college savings and a steady paycheck. He liked it better when soldiers showed up because their nation called them, a letter he priced at thirteen cents, with a draft-era requirement to show up for military service.

I wondered what Nunnelley and others like him might think about that same kid continuing to wear a uniform, and then a few decades later, getting notification of an eligibility to serve as a general officer. He was dubious about a group of one hundred and twenty lasting even ten weeks in uniform. He knew so much and represented the first of a trail of leaders that shaped my ability to serve, albeit with colorful language and the lack of expressed appreciation for our performance of duty.

I set down the phone and thought I would call Terry when the day was done to let her know. She could appreciate it with me; we could savor the moment. And then the unexpected news highlight would fade into oblivion, never to take shape in records or footsteps. A partner with her resolve and support over so many days when we were apart should know that without that foundation, I could have never continued to serve. She wrote me letters and recorded audio cassettes every day in Desert Storm. She tolerated the departures and the moments while I was physically there but not present. In overt ways and expressions to me, but far more in the way she sacrificed – many times in the background so that I could perform my duty – this process was enabled by our partnership. It was an imperfect path in many ways, complete with disagreements and conflict about incompatible schedules and time spent away from family. It didn't have to be that way. But it was, largely because of obligations that she accepted as ours and her willingness to walk alongside in that journey while at the same time picking up the slack at home. She was really the star.

As commander of the Army National Guard's only cyber brigade, there were nine hundred and eighty-five people in units in more than thirty states. We had recurring conferences and face-to-face meetings to synchronize activity and track top priorities. I attended a meeting at Fort Belvoir when the three star commander of Army Cyber Command asked to speak with me in the hallway. Left foot first to the hallway. Moving from the group, he was direct in asking if I would consider joining the command to work as the director of operations, first in Virginia and then leading its relocation to Georgia.

Although stunned by the invite, it was a simple yes from me with one hopeful caveat. I had only two months before accepted a position in the private sector with a major cyber security firm and asked if he would consider a phone call with my new boss, just to advocate the need for military leave. Having departed from my employer with mixed results previously, I wanted to ensure clear communication and intent for the request. He gladly agreed to make the call, and I expressed my sincere gratitude for the opportunity. The invite began the process of requesting orders. It would take some months.

The second consequential call was from Captain Kevin Spencer who greeted me with an unexpected opening line, saying, "My name

is Captain Spencer, and I am here to make you successful." His intro-
duction came as I prepared for the orders to begin in weeks at Fort
Belvoir. Kevin had been at the command, knew the role I would be
serving in, and had been the executive officer for the general officer
I would replace. He knew the processes and had finely tuned his actions
to support leaders.

In a small ceremony in Richmond, Virginia, the epaulets with one
star were first placed on my shoulders, an almost surreal milestone,
and one that gave me a few moments to speak. A red flag with one star
was unfurled for the first time, my command sergeant major and command chief warrant officer standing by my side. In brief comments,
I shared a piece of wisdom from a dear friend who served as a two-
star in the Marine Corps. "Wear it well, and use your star to help
other people," a simple guidepost for doing it right. And I reflected on
the enduring and resonant axiom from my father, "Don't cut yourself
shaving." Both were aimed at authentic leadership, selfless service, and
accountability to the team.

Kevin attended the ceremony, and when the donuts were done and
the audience faded, he met with me to give me a parking pass, unit
patches for my uniform, and his personal cell phone number to call
whenever needed. My career manager from my civilian employer met
me in the parking lot and shared my first salute in the new rank. I was
on military leave, but still in the conversation. We smiled talking about
the challenges ahead; I handed him my work laptop from the car trunk,
not knowing how long I would be away from the firm.

In the dizzying first days at Belvoir, I attended check-in meetings
with the entire staff and detailed sessions with the sections I would
oversee as the director of operations. For each one, Kevin had a printed
summary of attendees, purpose, and a clear description of any decision
that was required as a meeting outcome. These fit into a classified folder
and notebook that he routinely updated and locked in a vault when
the day was done. We were joined in partnership by an experienced
sergeant major, an extremely senior non-commissioned officer, whose

assignments all related to cyber, intelligence, and information technology. He was a powerhouse, as were many of similar rank, and could tackle issues with two phone calls or a stern glare.

The largest subordinate element to Army Cyber Command is located in Arizona, headquarters for the U.S. Army Network Enterprise Technology Command (NETCOM). Located in the middle of the desert, the long ride from the airport paired Kevin and I together for the coming days' sequence. This would be my first piece of travel with detailed briefings from the leadership and face-to-face meetings with several lieutenant colonels who were evaluated by me. The long flight from Washington, D.C., included a read-ahead packet of information with a robust calendar once we arrived.

At the installation, and after a full day of meetings, I was invited with another senior officer for dinner at the commander's home. Nervous about the invitation, I considered my gratitude for the warm invitation from the two-star invitee, a steady leader who synchronized the technology and inner workings of the Army's information network. Her historic quarters on post were impressive. Stepping across the threshold, I took stock of this cordial moment and the fact that a guy with my beginnings was invited.

After another day of meetings at NETCOM, Kevin and I ventured out for a late dinner to a place he lined up through a friend. We enjoyed some Cuban food, caught up on business between bites, and I gleaned a few more details about him in conversation. On the long ride back to our hotel, he asked me some questions about family, work, and other assignments. He asked more details about our youngest, a boy we had fostered and later adopted. He explored the topic where I explained how that process worked for us and what a blessing this had been to our family. I talked about how it made us grow in ways we never imagined. We parked efficiently, the vehicle neatly backed into its space, and walked to the lobby. We moved closer together, and I thought he was going to give me an executive summary of our schedule for the following day.

"The reason I asked is because I'm like Devin." I paused for a minute, realizing this was not a calendar update but a reference to our car conversation. When I stared in disbelief, he talked about his adoption, the brothers that he met later in life, and the parents who sewed together the jagged story of families torn apart. We lined up in that moment in a bit of common ground from two differing perspectives, but were now joined together. Two people, still in a hotel lobby, staring at one another. I took stock of this admirable young man and his maturity, poise, and the influence he had on others. I learned that it's okay to be known, to share deeply, and to listen to other people's stories.

Called to attend a conference in Arkansas, I departed from D.C. alone with a thick notebook and expectations of delivering comments to an executive board. Leaving instructions with my civilian deputy and the six colonels who worked in the shop, the Army was enabling updates to more than one million computer operating systems, an extremely complex alignment to ensure readiness and availability were not decremented. Their technical grit and months-long planning gave confidence that a brief trip was possible.

Landing in Little Rock, I checked voicemail, waiting on luggage. "Return immediately," was the directive. The return flight felt a little longer, mostly because the message was unable to give an unclassified reason for the recall. Pacing the stairs to the basement-level sensitive compartmented information facility (SCIF), the operations center was buzzing with activity, screens showing collaboration with the Middle East. In the hours that followed, Qasem Soleimani, an Iranian major general, was killed by an American drone strike near Baghdad International Airport.

Once in Georgia, the command envisioned an Information Warfare Operations Center in a brand-new facility and with a design indicative of the inaugural name, context, and function. Walls of knowledge, immense screens tied to computer systems, surrounded the chairs and arrangements of a world-class operations center. The building footprint created more than three hundred thousand square feet of workspace.

Fiber connecting computer systems could be measured in hundreds of miles. More than five hundred whiteboards were placed near work spaces. Less than ten people had assigned seats. Collaboration was baked into its construct, a critical element in a new and dynamic space for cyber, electronic warfare, and information operations.

Captain Spencer traveled to Georgia, and with my senior enlisted advisor, set up the meeting cadence and scheme for our initial weeks at the new location. They exchanged critical details for daily requirements, notebook preparation, business process and key relationships. With good fortune, I was soon assigned a new aide, an extremely sharp cyber officer, Nate McFadden, who had a degree in computer science and deep technical chops. He sustained the momentum gained in previous months duty and ably assisted in the brand new space.

The novelty of the new position had not worn off. Parking in a marked spot and navigating through secure gates with codes, I could look to the building's glass front and see a flag pole flying a one-star flag, representing my role and presence. Imposter syndrome: How did I get picked for this, and can anyone tell that I don't know as much as I should? I reconciled my truth, that timing more than talent led to my selection. The certificate that made me eligible came a year after my first application was not accepted. Not all my evaluations were top block with glowing comments. I was privileged to work with professionals who enabled any success and quickly addressed shortfalls and mistakes. This rank was not mine; I was wearing team colors. I prayed I would be faithful to that calling.

Less than two hundred and twenty flag officers serve in the Army during any one given time. A scarce few were added above that congressionally mandated level, but only because of critical operational requirements, and those additional flag officers came from the Army National Guard and Army Reserve. Coming from the sidelines into active duty, abundant restrictions on their duty were limited to no more than six-month tours. My orders were renewed three times. Considering the odds, selection rates for promotion dwindled considerably above major, three grades below my unexpected promotion. My appreciation was great, as was my hesitation.

A fundamental requirement in my duties was to enable and develop leaders assigned within the directorate. Six full colonels and almost twenty lieutenant colonels were in my "rating chain" for performance evaluations that were central to their current and future success. The stakes in writing these reports were raised considerably, certainly by volume, but also with a vast difference within active-duty ranks. Reserve component service members appreciate the reports, but they are likely not core to their livelihood and primary means of living. Noting the difference, I invested the time to learn subtle changes in lexicon, form, and function in writing these critical reports. Nate created a valuable spreadsheet and scheduled quarterly video teleconferences, so even the officers I rated that served in overseas locations could be fairly evaluated.

At times, I felt like a stranger planted in the middle of a technically fluent and functioning team. My bias, from enlisted beginnings and extensive time in the private sector, collided at times with cultural norms and the small circle of expectations. The person sitting at the end of the table does not always have the answer. Experts exist on many levels, and rank is not always indicative of where solutions can be found. PowerPoint is not the cumulative sum of all we know, and answering emails does not measure completion or communication. Asking questions, even challenging group sentiment, proves to find more answers and builds collective ingenuity.

Because my technical grit was not as deep, I leaned into people and processes. Where I did not fully understand the binary and forensics, I could reinforce the experts and clear their obstacles. Leveraging a myriad of failures and shortfalls in my career, I had learned to be a multiplier, a leader who could add momentum. It was difficult to resist my own "Good Idea Fairy" tendencies. The tour confirmed the catchphrase for effective leaders that "no one cares what you know until they know how much you care."

Routinely waking early, and then earlier as the tempo and mission demands increased in the months since my appointment, the effectiveness of the Peloton to burn off anxiety was diluted over time. Not for lack of my sustained interest in the bike, but for the palpable changes in my ability to absorb the stress. I learned my need for some time of reflection and movement in my mornings before landing in the vortex of work requirements. The intensity and level of responsibility was daunting: global activity and deployed soldiers, critical capability, and an algebraic increase in cyber activity and attacks. The notebook had to be digested, distilled to make effective decisions, a weight felt internally that I tried to balance with exercise and solitude.

A completely different circle of connections existed within the flag officer ranks. High performing individuals who traded their hard work in successively difficult positions had earned a network of associates. Decisions impacting the Army and critical to operations were navigated through their interactions with an expectation that disagreement would only occur in small groups, providing decision space to accommodate where possible. Talented and intense, I wondered at times if they saw my stripes or if I was meeting the grade.

The last phone call related to being a general was in the form of a secure one-to-one video call conducted over a classified video teleconference. I had made the meeting request with the director of the NSA, who also served as the commander of U.S. Cyber Command. I did so with hesitation and realistic expectations that a four-star with his responsibilities was too busy for a meeting without obvious correlation to current priorities. I created a draft email to send when the request was not accepted.

In the conference room, Nate set up the meeting. He conducted the confirmation of the secure channel and departed, leaving me alone. He zoomed in the camera so I could be seen, although solo, at the end of a conference table with seats for twenty. I turned to my personal notes, saw the three headlines of my intentions, and waited for the screen to show a familiar face.

I began expressing my sincere appreciation for him taking the meeting, one that was trivial relative to his assignments and critical operational requirements. I had the chance to characterize what I saw as the cascading impact of bold decisions he made three years earlier with Task Force Echo. His decision to resource extensive training was an investment that delivered consequence for this mission but enabled the formation, and soldiers, to gain amazing training and certifications. In more than three years of sustained involuntary mobilizations, the retention rate remained above ninety percent, a novelty and envious position for the new organization. Leaders who saw beyond the existing model and complexity made decisions that informed an exciting future.

I took a deep breath before telling him how grateful I was to have served. And I was more candid in telling him that I believed it was the comments he wrote in an evaluation report that allowed me through a narrow window to be promoted. Simple phrases in less than two sentences made all the difference. He paused, commenting on amazing soldiers, and replied it was not simply the words but likely footsteps that led to another opportunity to serve. We ended the call moments later, the last classified connection of my career, and one I would savor for a lifetime.

Days later, Nate drove us to Fort Bragg where I would out-process and work the administrative processes to separate from the uniform. In an odd circumstance and pairing, we departed the operations center to drive more than four hours during a large-scale cyber incident that paralyzed the East Coast gasoline supplies. He had carefully planned our route with stations and places where he knew we could refuel.

The old building where the administrative offices were located was a short walk from "Green Ramp," the large hangar and gathering point where airborne operations took place. Rows of large planes that carried passengers who exited mid-air from the side door were arranged in layers. C-130 aircraft were essential to the one-way ticket into the sky. The flight line roared in the background with Air Force planes sustaining their day-by-day mission without pause. I took a seat in the waiting room, and Nate checked us in for appointments with each section for securing my discharge. The office was also responsible for departing soldiers, those called to deploy. The juxtaposition provided a meaningful picture of our taxed and valuable forces, those called forward and those moving into the next chapter.

Having refueled the car with the rationed gallons allowed, we grabbed a sandwich, and I asked Nate to drive to the other side of post. I wanted him to see H4822, the barracks where I lived when I first joined the Army, one that I wondered if still existed or had been bulldozed almost forty years later. The parking lot showed the most evidence of age, reduced to broken asphalt and stripes that were no longer visible. The pay phone where I occasionally called home was gone. The bus stop that took me to the airfield had been taken away.

I asked Nate to join me when we stepped out to see the barracks and look to the third story resting spot that was my home when this all started. He moved to my left, abiding a protocol for accompanying a senior officer, and we stepped across the winding cracked sidewalk to stand at the bottom of the stairs. The building exterior was largely unchanged, save for new signs indicating the unit and current tenant.

I smiled with Nate and asked for a selfie to savor, one to remember a day of reflection, a punctuation mark for the journal and a keepsake of my time in uniform.

In a small auditorium inside the NSA Georgia facility, members of my family were invited by exception to join a brief ceremony and reception. My three-star boss presided and shared his comments, words that I savored from an authentic and seasoned leader whose trust never eroded, even when results were less satisfying in my estimation. I shared the story of E31, the inspiring character of Air Assault School who was emblematic of the passion and purpose of our Armed Forces. I felt fortunate that my family got to meet the people and faces from recent years serving and hear some insights for our collective work in unspoken spaces. I attempted to verbalize gratitude to my family and felt the full weight of their sacrifices, recognizing my incomplete ability to articulate its meaning. The debt I owed to those seated and others in decades before was great, and no continuance of comments or ceremony could bridge that gap.

CHAPTER 15

Amy's Office

"TAKE A LEFT IN THE hallway, and my office is there at the end." And so began the first visit with Amy, a trained counselor who specializes in stressor-related anxiety disorders. I had waited for several weeks to get the appointment, and at some level, it felt like I had waited years to get in this seat.

Amy began her interview with some description of responses that we have as humans. She was trying to teach me about our body's anxiety response. And then in even more detail, she told the story of the fox. She described the fox who saw the coyote, a natural enemy. Once seen, the fox immediately sought refuge and sprinted to nearby trees and a vantage point to see he was clear of the coyote. His legs moved at their fastest pace, the fox drew breath and energy from instinct knowing that not being fast enough, not escaping the view of the coyote would mean certain death.

The fox continued to run and to hide until it looked over the green grass and no longer saw the predator. The fox smelled for the coyote, listened for the coyote, and looked again. And when there was no predator to be seen, the fox settled again into his exploration for food. There was no memory of the chase, his breath went back to normal, and the fears that drove his quick speed to escape disappeared. It was over.

To be an animal brain, Amy explained, was to naturally possess the ability to turn down the fear response once it was obvious there was nothing to fear. She described how our human brain has a component that performs in that same way. Except for some, the fight-or-flight instinct gets turned on, and no message travels to the animal brain to let it know that fear may no longer be required. This is me and indicative of many who suffer from PTSD. Instead of turning it off, this conflict is not resolved, and the human continues to deliver energy to the body to respond. Cortisol is sent to the body, the heart rate increases, blood rushes to the limbs, and the alertness drives instinctive responses. Attempting to make it stop created anger. This explained, at least in part, how my body was stuck on startle and could not take in sounds, inputs, or fear without running from the coyote.

Oddly, I felt guilt about the way that I responded.

In this first session with Amy, she asked for my goals and hopes for our time together. I asked for peace and a way to respond normally to the world around me. Certainly, there were things in my life that were consequences, but to the extent I knew intellectually that the trauma had passed, I had lost an ability to calm my primal fear.

I took the following appointments in weekly increments to share parcels of what sparked my responses and led to remnants of fear. I talked about the blast of artillery firing in Desert Storm and the night I jumped into a shallow pit. I described the faces of Iraqi children who cried when burns and wounds were treated by our medics. My trust for a counselor had grown, and I shared the shame I felt for being so weak in such a moment. I told her how foolish I felt being reduced to my shaky self whenever a noise was heard.

Calmly, Amy explained that my responses, the fear that caused me to dive into the sand for cover, were natural and were correct. Years of training reinforced the response. The fear was required and actually saved my life. I had never considered that possibility. She explained that jumping for cover when you think artillery is going to hit your position is the right action, the perfect life-preserving response to a situation when life seemed threatened.

Knowing more about the brain stem and my fear response did not change anything. The intellectual truth was of no consequence. I saw myself shining a light on one part of the problem, when another circumstance provided a foothold for later problems. The need for my younger self to be free of guilt and shame was part of what I was trying to preserve later in life. I would have to share that secret with Amy to move ahead.

On a soft chair in her office, she asked about my journaling and ways that I had considered to outline the details of my story. She wanted it to have details for our work together, but more importantly, she knew that documenting my journey would provide a useful outlet. And, she agreed, we could keep that writing secret. Still.

I told her I had written a poem, something she agreed was a different approach to journaling. I described the night I actively considered my own death, awoken by a recurring dream that haunted me. It was the first time I saw a root in a tree of despair. There was no song or lyrics that could explain the abuse that happened when I was young.

Amy's appreciation for the poem was not for its lyrical blend of poetry and rhyming sophistication. If there was any. She was far more enlightened by seeing this foundation, a violation that occurred as a child that continued to invade my thoughts of who I am as an adult.

She asked permission to ask me some of my favorite things, remembrances, or objects that I perceived as peaceful and calm. I shared my wonder for the sunrise, the light slowly erupting from the horizon and making its way to warm us. She asked for a smell or aroma that was a reminder of something pleasant and an image that conveyed calm. In a guided meditation, she slowly narrated brief sentences, illuminating a scene: I was calmly standing in water as the sun rose in the distance. The light reflected on the water's surface, a salmon sky coming to life from the sun's slow rise, waking birds and causing a slight breeze. Her steady delivery described my feet slowly touching the water without hesitation and notice of the temperature. The air moved to help me notice the aroma of fresh blooms and moisture.

It was minutes into her meditation that brought me into the water above my waist, calmly enjoying being surrounded by still water. My hands could move, she suggested, and could push the water to make my body swim. She slowed the descriptive pace of her monologue to describe what I saw, the first wave of water created from calm and gently moved by my arms. I should see the wave create a concentric circle. The first wave moved ahead of me. And then the second, but each one in echelon and accord with the first. A growing set of circles patterned in the water and glistened with the rising sun.

The scene and her peaceful voice were calming and slow. In focusing on the narrative, I was taken to an imaginary place where there was safety. I felt the significance of the wave beginning with my arm movement and creating layers to my front. This was calm reassurance. I was welcome there.

In future sessions, she changed the context and encouraged my use of mindfulness, the slow appreciation for a scene or real-life experience that we slowly described to ourselves.

Coming back to the poem, she asked permission for a time to imagine the boy I once was and to see him at a distance. I understood conceptually that such a meditation would fit into a model just like the calm water. Even so, I was unable to see that person at a distance. I could imagine what he saw but could not fully grasp the other viewpoint. I saw that I remained a prisoner to the shelter of my own perspectives. Amy wanted these two characters to be closer, perhaps to reconcile or learn from. I naturally preferred peace.

Appointments from the military hospital and care from behavioral health were all absorbed by the Veterans Administration (VA). They offered assignment to a clinic focused on veterans from recent conflicts and were tuned into their specific needs. Hearing aids were updated to include Bluetooth capability, a feature that was not allowed inside classified spaces. Medicines easily crossed over and assessments for behavioral health and primary care were assigned.

Psychiatry met face to face to describe my symptoms and ways to make it better. A blend of prescriptions could lower the anxiety threshold, although calibrating dosage would take some time. In the two-week follow up, my comment that I was not sleeping well sparked another prescription: sleeping pills to ensure I could rest. Made dull by the combination, I could not rest with the prospect of recovering and moving forward while ingesting pills. I saw another addiction.

Cognitive Behavioral Therapy was suggested as the gold standard for working through trauma, a four-month out-patient program of intense counseling, journaling, and reflection. My guide was a younger trained counselor whose father had suffered from PTSD returning from Vietnam. His ability to listen made safe harbor in sessions where we worked through a workbook of assignments. Disliking portions of the homework, I channeled more energy into writing a book.

The centerpiece of journaling was the description of events that ceded the trauma, called the "stressor statement." I felt no need to edit, but in sessions read it aloud while the counselor carefully dissected descriptions of my perceptions. He carefully asked for permission to review it with me. Although it was not intended as scrutiny, it was difficult to slowly work through the details and my broken recollection. It was unsatisfying in that words did not capture all the ingredients, and the dialogue sparked moments of silence. Even an incomplete exercise fueled my sense that I could not explain its entirety and perhaps doing so would never eliminate the sparks caused by sounds. Only my brain stem could do that.

Cognitive Behavioral Therapy aims to promote knowledge of the gap between what we perceive or feel and the factual evidence in our environment. Conditions and circumstances can trigger feelings that could be without basis. Accepting that truth, my journal worked through scenarios where I was sparked in one direction, with little evidence confirming feelings. Perhaps people near me were pleasant, maybe no one sees what triggers me. Knowing there was a correlation was helpful, but none of the program would eliminate the possibility of sudden sounds and movement in my life. In a valuable observation, returning to the clinic and even the parking lot, I saw the roaming platoon of veterans who had needs and also support. I was not alone. The program may have not solved the puzzle, but there were fewer pieces to go. Or maybe this winding road would continue with an equal appreciation for moments of peace and the journey itself.

CHAPTER 16

Into the Cold

SWEAT FORMED ON MY HEAD as I inhaled deeply and then exhaled completely without pause, a slow cadence and tempo set by the voice from Kyle's phone. He played a clip from Wim Hof, an athlete and guru whose study of Tibetan meditation and eastern practice had led him to promote breathing exercises. I continued in parallel with the direction and felt my body move when the air filled my lungs and diaphragm. Waves of vibration went to my arms, a slow buzzing caused by the oxygenation and blood flow to capillaries. My head felt like it was moving in a slow rhythm, and my temperature increased. I sensed I was lifting up. When the count stopped, I closed my mouth, waiting for the time to elapse and focusing on relaxing during the pause. Having increased my breath volume, my body was filled with oxygen, and I felt no urge to breathe. I wasn't holding my breath; instead, I was relying on my body to pause with the fuel onboarded with repeated breath. Full and feeling calm, I leaned into the quiet and let my body adjust to the time. The "not breathing and hold" easily went for more than a minute and passed quickly. The voice chimed in, "Take a deep breath and hold for fifteen seconds," ending the exercise and giving me a rush of calm energy.

Driving to the pickleball court, I turned on our familiar route from our neighborhood and into the adjacent streets. Our conversation was in a pause as we anticipated another morning to see this senior group of players who invited our participation in the twice weekly games. The rotation of players and their friendly style drew us to enjoy doubles and learn that power was not the only way to score points. The strategy and precision of their pickleball game play was in contrast to our more bombastic approach. We slapped the ball, hoping to spin it with the paddle and push it past opponents. This worked when we played singles but was refuted by their simple return and placement.

Georgia summers necessarily led to the early morning schedule so heat would not be a concern. We had our backpack with paddles, extra balls, and water to refresh us in the two hours of activity. Looking ahead, I saw the stop sign at the base of the hill leading to the community pickleball courts. My body convulsed and shook when the phone rang through the stereo, a hands-free setting that was much louder than music. The ringing overtook the car and all my being. When the phone rang, it was transferred to the car stereo. The sound sent electricity through me in an uncontrolled response that pushed me into the steering wheel, letting go as my hand reached for the window. I convulsed as the ring sounded the second time, losing control of the car and barely getting my foot to smash the brake.

Kyle and I were now over the curb, the car stopped and my head spinning while I gasped for breath. He reached for the wheel and held it tightly so we did not lose control. My mind felt riddled with marbles that were spinning, colliding, and bouncing from within. I felt lost and heard groans and noises ooze from my mouth without any intention. I inhaled slightly, feeling my heart race, and knew what had happened. Immediately ashamed, I was lost again. My eyes filled with tears as I attempted to answer pleas asking if I was okay. His hand touched my shoulder, and I came to terms with what had happened, a bolt that took me from reality into a PTSD response. Sweat formed on my head, and my thumping heart began to slow with his calming words and firm touch.

Stunned by the event, I took a breath to clear the moment and grabbed the wheel to get the car moving again. My hands trembled, and I felt guilty for putting us at risk, all for the sound that launched the episode. Ascending the hill, I turned into the community parking lot next to the pickleball courts. I took a moment to gain composure, again hearing Kyle query my condition. "I really think breathing could help you, Dad." In the weeks previous, he had sent me links to videos where breathing exercises were used to lower anxiety. I ignored them completely by agreeing in principle that breathing could work, but not accepting it would help me. Maybe that was a method for someone else. He had explored the technique and shared that it was powerful as a natural tool. I had the bag of prescription solutions from the VA, and my weeks-long trial with those answers came up short.

Joined in the car now, having completed the exercise, I looked to Kyle to thank him for leading me to this drill and a way to break out of the anxiety. As much as the episodes frustrated me with their unpredictable timing, I saw a new tool for PTSD that could enhance my recovery.

Part of the Wim Hof approach includes immersion in cold water. In December, conditions offered the prospect of getting into our pool with outdoor temperatures in the 40s and a pool water temperature of 52 degrees. As I stepped into the water, I realized my own resistance to the idea the moment my foot first touched the water and reached my ankles. Knowing I had to push further, I stumbled forward, landing in the three-foot height, paralyzed by the shocking cold. The breath that I tried to hold and slowly release came out in the form of a primal grunt, a painful exasperation and cry that forced me to inhale again and gasp for the courage to kneel.

With water up to my chin, I exhaled, feeling the cold snap and sting my arms and legs. I captured another breath, and the wave caused by my immersion lessened, and the water grew still. My struggle to resist parted, and the water calmed. I closed my eyes, feeling the anguish in submitting to the extreme but imagining that the feeling could not get worse. Another breath. Slowing my heart rate, I remained still, taking in the cold and considering how the seconds kept ticking. After a short period, I felt the slight warmth of water by my sides magically creating heat from my body. A thermal layer formed around my submerged body. I committed to being still and marveled at the way my body naturally responded to the stress. My body created heat, small changes in the water surrounding me, giving me a sense that I was winning a battle.

The thermal layer was a picture of my journey. My meditation grew deeper with gratitude for this minute change, the slightest difference next to my skin. The water could get no colder. Time was moving ahead and the remaining time needed in immersion was growing smaller. Kneeling in the calm, I carefully thought of each of my children. I visualized their faces and concentrated my prayer for them, my gratitude for how God cared for them. I prayed new prayers for each, now considering my experience kneeling in church growing up and seeing this moment to reflect. With prayers completed, I opened my eyes slightly, squinting to see the light reflect from the pool. The green from nearby trees and the shadow of tall pines were sketched in the water. I felt I saw the colors more clearly in my calm.

The watch alarm began marking three minutes, and I moved quickly from the blanket of almost warm water that surrounded me and quickly raced out of the pool. Standing with a towel and looking at Kyle, I smiled thinking I could stand outside without a towel and never truly be cold again.

In the days to come, I grew more faithful to the practice of cold water, using it simply as a way to see my body naturally push against its challenges. I drew meaning from its powerful energy, not in strength as measured by muscles but by the magnitude of its response and capability. The deep breathing that drew oxygen to my core calmed me and elevated my outlook. The cold stimulation of the water presented an obstacle that I could overcome daily. Testing and building my resilience. It was that simple.

My body was created with an ability to solve these natural problems. I resisted the cold water and made excuses for why I should wait longer, prepare myself more, or set conditions where I would like getting in. My dislike for the shock did not subside, and my resistance and eventual accomplishment became a victory. And to my amazement, my body almost celebrated the energy drawn from the cold. Exhilaration and brightness covered me. It lasted for hours.

The mechanics of the cold are worth understanding. I learned it was not simply a stunt, some trick or dare where I jumped into the pool. The process created far more robust results. Cold water immersion can indeed evoke exhilarating sensations, both physiologically and psychologically. When individuals engage in activities like cold water exposure, they often experience a surge of adrenaline, noradrenaline, and cortisol due to the cold shock response. This sudden drop in skin temperature triggers a cascade of hormonal reactions, leading to heightened alertness and a sense of achievement. Cortisol is also transmitted through the body in a fear or startle response. Channeling this natural ingredient for wellness was a powerful tool I could enlist without a prescription. In the water, I found a way to push against the seemingly random and persistent drag of PTSD and depression.

There is rightful concern about the number of veterans who take their own lives. Aside from the startling reality that in 2022 seventeen former military members took their lives every day, the infection has grown exponentially in our country. If we add the veteran populations' suicide statistics to active military, we find alarming losses. In fact, the age-adjusted suicide rate increased by more than four percent in an eight-year period (2014-2022), making it the second leading cause of death for people age 10-34.

The stark numbers have received attention in that the topic of suicide is now openly discussed. Recognizing the problem, each of the services have dedicated training and programs to address the issue, focused on teaching resilience. The ability to work through a dark cloud is essential to getting beyond the tyranny of the current problem and seeing into another day.

Sui is the Latin word for "self," and the remainder of the word "suicide" means "to slay." So, with this etymology in mind, there is the picture of self-killing one's self. Although true to its Latin root, the more contemporary context has to do with hopelessness. One misperception to many who have not internalized this struggle is when you hear, "it's a cry for help." Suicidal ideations are different for everyone, but the persistent theme that it's an appeal seems flawed. My own sense in that dark time was to get relief, to escape, and to end the suffering. "Help" would imply that someone wanted others to be involved in response. That was not my perspective. In fact, quite to the contrary.[1]

As a leader in the military, I participated in prescribed suicide prevention classes annually and saw the intent to provide the information was factual, compassionate, and professional. Considering my own suicidal ideations, I confess, I never shared my truth with other leaders and those near me. This failure to be authentic is endemic to the culture that has an expectation for toughness but does not see how strength is built. There remains fear of the stigma associated with needing help.

Strong muscles require exercise, sometimes taxing a muscle to its limit. Then there is rest and recovery. Refuel. New goals and variety in exercises build capacity from the last routine. There may be injuries and time for pause to recover fully. Training to become more physical is not a linear means to accumulate strength by adding more and more weight, more distance, and more intensity. Instead, there is a sine wave of accomplishment that includes failure. As a culture, we seem unwilling to accept this truth: success is not always built on success. Real success is best informed by failure; frequently, the mistakes we hate most, we later call experience. The two conditions are tied together in an equation where the character determines what they do and how they respond to the failure, the pause and mistakes that are organic to our experience.

---

1   https://www.ptsd.va.gov/professional/treat/cooccurring/suicide_ptsd.asp

It's this parity, the battle to be successful and the truth that it doesn't come easy and often, that can paralyze us, and that appears to be evidenced in the military and particularly with young people. Stigma, the assignment of a negative attribute to an individual, is a strong cultural factor in military circles. As a person who had agency with some of those people, I regret not taking an opportunity to share more openly, when appropriate. They may have learned from my struggles. We talked about lessons learned, but I failed to share my insight.

I have imagined what I might say, not wanting to be persuasive as much as to be seen as telling my truth. We can learn from other people's trials, and that vulnerability and perspective might disrupt the stereotype we have built around being perfect and how we achieve happiness. Perhaps standing up in testimony would help eliminate the stigma of feeling helpless.

If I had the chance, this is what I would say. Without a microphone and without a podium:

"I thought you should know something about me, about my past, and about how I learned to move forward when things got tough. I faced adversity, just like many of you, challenges that overtook me in the moment and were devastating. I experienced loss, like many of you, and frankly, I had doubts about how I could ever work through the sadness. I've experienced family deaths, experienced disappointments, and been kicked in the ass. Combat and the insanity of war makes deep imprints in people. Honestly, sharing that experience with brothers is something I treasure. Something so jagged cuts through many layers and ties us together. Misery can do that. I feel fortunate to have served with heroes. Perhaps you feel that fellowship. Sadly, I also remember scenes I wish I could un-see. Sounds disrupt my normal. Fear comes back to me and drags me back to conflict and the toughest moments. This condition weathers me in ways I have yet to understand.

My truth is, I lost my way. Clouds filled my morning.

I had days where I was in the shadow, fighting nightmares and anxiety that would not go away. I was receding. My body changed and became dull. I existed, but I lost my grip on meaning. I was hopeless and afraid. I did not know the way out. I wanted out. Badly. Yes, that badly.

We convince ourselves that we should do the right things, achieve the next goal, and move forward. This is baked into our understanding of promotions, titles, and responsibility. But what we seem to miss is our humanity as imperfect beings, capable of many things but subject to the frailties of both our bodies and mind. We fail sometimes. We get kicked in the ass and are hurt, not knowing how to get up and try again. There are things we cannot do.

We celebrate progression and recognition in our culture, and this evolution likely appears like a moving sidewalk. You enter at one level, and as time passes and you complete tasks, you arrive at the next rank, the next job, and the next reward. We talk too little about failing. We are taught that we must perform tasks to standard and have little appreciation for failure as a way to learn and improve. We look at a person with titles and positions higher than us and imagine they have some skill or attribute that makes them better. That is fake. It's fake that senior leaders are without error, and it's untrue that they arrived at their elevated role without failure.

I wish I had raised my hand when I first felt like I should take my life and leave this Earth. But I hunkered down in my private space. I became fascinated with my own death and leaned into a painful dark spiral that hurt and made me a prisoner to my thoughts of suicide. I believe God provided a light to me, extending an opportunity for me to see the hand of a person in my life who reached out, without judgment or disdain to help pull me up. The truth is, I didn't know where I was going, but I knew it was time to get up. I grabbed his hand as I imagined it and slowly began a journey from darkness. I moved forward imperfectly, but I moved.

As difficult as our experience can be at times, you deserve to have testimony of someone who has been in the storm. I regret it has taken me this long to stand before you and share it. I regret that suicide is such a recurring lightning bolt to our loved ones that we struggle to confront. I don't have the solutions. I have an experience that I needed to share. I have a sincere hope that you see support around you and not the facade of perfect leaders who somehow evolved without dents, scratches, and dark challenges to their happiness and meaning in life. We all search for meaning, the notion that what we are doing has consequence and value to others. We can consider who we are and find ways to accept the ups and painful downs.

Finally, I care about you. I care that you are okay. I care that you see a hand of support when you need it. It's here. Your circle is willing to join you. We're on the same team.

It's an emergency. A mostly invisible demon is getting inside our best and brightest and extinguishing their flame. We need to come to terms with that truth. We must do something different to make it go away. Videos alone won't get us there. We need you, and you, and you. We should aspire for a trust that includes misfortune. It's been said we can color with broken crayons. It's time to do that. Urgently and genuinely. Be stirred to action. Be moved from the comfort of pointing somewhere else. My testimony is a fraction of what reality really is.

We picked all the cool kids to be on our team, and that worked in grade school. Today, our team includes everyone. We owe one another support. A hand to reach, a voice in the silence, and a way to see how we are connected. As tragic as losses from suicide always will be, perhaps the more startling truth is that shining light into hopelessness is not that hard. Or better said, we make it harder than it should be. God gave us two ears and only one mouth. That's a practical way to maybe see what comes first: listening.

Farmers learn something important that technology and innovation cannot change: If you want to harvest corn in August, you must plant in May. You can change how you add water, and you can use fertilizer. But corn grows over a long time. That is the way that corn seeds are when they are planted in soil. And this is the way our deepest relationships work. They take time, good soil, moisture, and elimination of weeds. Give that some thought: the strong interest we should have in actually knowing our teammates and the reality that relationships season. You can't put it in the microwave to heat it up faster. No app to click on to make your footsteps less critical. So let us learn from the farmer: plant now what you plan to reap in the future. Prepare your hands and heart now to be ready when it's time. It must be time."

Amidst the blur of mentions with PTSD is the fundamental confusion over what it is and is not. Certainly, there are many forms of trauma. One of the common misperceptions is that trauma can be differentiated from one person to another. That is to suggest that different people experiencing the same circumstance internalize it differently. This is a stereotype that I hear often in social circles, a belief that one person as a multiple combat tour veteran has "real" PTSD and somehow the person with less deployed experience, less violence, or another challenge may rate lower in the scale. While it is true that PTSD appears to have different ways that it inhibits people's normal existence, we cannot dismiss the non-combatant silent wound.

In my case, the best way that I understand PTSD is to emphasize the word "disorder." I was diagnosed with PTSD in a medical screening and had it confirmed over a period of twenty years. I experienced bouts with anger, had nightmares, and fell into spells of depression. But it was not until the last three years that I felt my "order" was no longer functioning. The brain stem response to sounds alerted to a fight-or-flight response. This was an instinctual response based on my internal panic with sounds and surprise. My fight or flight button was broken. These conditions raised my concern that I was not simply troubled and occasionally prone to alert, but in fact, there were times when I was in danger of being hurt as a result of my response. And the worst part, there was little that could be done immediately to make it better.

Drugs were the primary mode relied upon by the VA, but the levels needed to dull this response negatively impacted the quality of my life. Brain stems do not have a lasting response to Prozac. Sleeping pills don't help nightmares. Even so, I departed from the clinic with a full bag, along with sleep aids and a complex plan of taking, eating, and documenting progress. I took them as the doctors ordered. In doing so, I stepped into the fog and wondered how it was that I was now on the sidelines, passively watching my life exist without me. I wondered when I would find one that worked, and if it did, if I would pass the test and resist abusing it like I had other medicines. Should I just fill the pill box weekly and accept this new existence?

Amyotrophic Lateral Sclerosis (ALS) is a horrific and long-lasting disease better known by the famous baseball player Lou Gehrig, who died from it in 1941. Researchers continue to study the complex disease and ways to provide remedy. Some years ago, social media took on the storm of the "ALS Ice Challenge," a video contest where one person poured ice over their head and then challenged another to do the same. It went viral. The challenge was widely popular and raised awareness for important research and funding. Looking back, the ice challenge was clearly a gimmick, a chance for someone to get attention for their iced response. Cold ice poured over someone's head focused the observer on the social media post, but many who posted were first interested in their own recognition, wanting to gain likes, shares, and attention. It worked, and the phenomenon drew more attention that attracted a fourfold increase in federal funding for research, from less than fifty million annually in 2015 to more than two hundred million in 2023.

What will be the consequence of the "22-per-day" push-up challenge? In imitating the ALS effort, attempting to draw similar viral results, people video themselves completing twenty-two push-ups and post it to social media with a mention of the number of veterans who commit suicide each day. Twenty-two. The stark reality of eight thousand people dying each year deserves attention.

Is doing push-ups getting to the root and providing a focus on individuals and a segment of our society struggling with hopelessness? Perhaps it is too early to tell. Perhaps this demonstration begins a conversation. Or perhaps we remain unwilling to move beyond the attention seeking efforts and into an authentic dialogue about the magnitude and scope of darkness and how people die without help.

Although ALS and suicide have little in common, they share an audience that aspires to draw attention to the problem. For ALS, that has resulted in increased funding and medical research with an objective of finding a cure, likely enabled by drugs and pharmaceutical interventions. In contrast, combatting suicide may not be solely found in medicines and pills. In fact, mental and spiritual wellness can be achieved and maintained without the pills. Many would argue the pills only further complicate the problem. As a result, it could be that incentives for major pharmaceutical companies and business would be less present with suicide. Another argument balancing that statement would be that diseases like ALS have a diagnosis while suicide is considered an event, even though we understand it is many times associated with mental health.

Having no medical background, I consider the evidence of my own experience entering the medical system with reports from many dear friends who share a similar report. The cliché is that "if you are a hammer, everything you see is a nail." Along that line, if we continue to approach mental wellness with a bias that prescriptions alone are solutions, then we fail to see a myriad of other solutions and approaches.

And it's clear, for now, that missing full consideration of those options is leading to the status quo we dislike today.

The suicide rate per 100,000 service members was 28.9 in the Army, 20.6 in the Navy, and 19.7 in the Air Force; no one died by suicide in the Space Force, according to the Pentagon's data.[2]

From 2001 through 2021, suicide rates increased most years for males and females. The total age-adjusted suicide rate increased from 10.7 deaths per 100,000 standard population in 2001 to a recent peak of 14.2 in 2018, and then declined to 13.5 in 2020.[3]

Despite the chaos, funds began to make their way to the ALS community a month after the challenge went viral. As a result, ALS treatment clinics in the U.S. nearly doubled, and funding from the U.S. National Institutes of Health rose from $49 million a year in 2015 to a projected $220 million in 2024.[4]

In my last two years in uniform, I reported early to prepare for the day and briefed senior leaders on the most up-to-date information. Given that these reports were due at 7:00 a.m., I made a routine of getting up at 4:30 a.m. so I could drink a cup of coffee, give myself a few moments of quiet, and then get to the Peloton bike for exercise. Making the adjustment to the early start was difficult at first, but it was a trade worth making because I knew physical exertion had a part in lowering my stress. Getting to bed by 9:00 p.m. was not always convenient, but doing that allowed me to build some space in the morning.

The first cup of coffee was the one I enjoyed most. The caffeine spark and warm drink in my hand was something to look forward to, even on the days when it was hardest to hear the alarm. It was spring when I felt

2   https://www.marinecorpstimes.com/news/your-marine-corps/2023/11/13/ marines-grapple-with-highest-suicide-rate-of-all-us-military-services/.

3   https://www.cdc.gov/nchs/products/databriefs/db464.htm.

4   https://www.nationalgeographic.com/science/article/als-ice-bucket-challenge -research-impact.

the first stings of depression that seemed to arrive without warning. The morning cup was full, no major obstacles were in front of me, and for all appearances, it was just another day. With my iPad in hand, I had scrolled from the verse of the day, to the news, and then to videos.

I found myself completing one video and being prompted to see the next, a short video displaying the Old Guard at Arlington Cemetery. They marched the Tomb of the Unknown Soldier with precision. I watched another, and then clicked another. Each one added to a sadness that I felt for death, for the ones who had died and those who were there to pay their respects. Tears covered me, and in the quiet morning before the coffee was finished and the day began, I wept. With another morning came the same sense of sadness, a cloudy time familiar to me and one that haunted my sense of wellness.

Because I left for work before the sunrise most days, I had little room to take my son, Devin, to school. His classes began at 8:00 a.m., and by that time, I was already in my third meeting for the day. There were a few occasions where I took him to an appointment or there was a way that our schedules aligned so I could be his ride to school. Knowing he would take some time to rise, I stopped in his room before I exercised. And then again after, encouraging him to get a shower and be ready soon. Once more before I shaved, and now with clarity that we had to leave in twelve minutes. Stepping upstairs, I felt my impatience boiling when I opened the door to his room. In a gravel-voiced outburst, I shouted at him until he was awake, seeing his eyes look at me in fear when he saw my red face leaning into him with expletives and anger. Feeling the rage take me over, I stood upright before the sweat began to form on my forehead. With one last burst of anger, I grabbed the doorknob and moved to the hallway.

With heavy breathing, I felt my heart race as I touched my head and the sweat that formed above my eyebrow. Shame overtook me, and I winced thinking of my verbal tirade and the scared eyes of my son. My day had been ambushed by a rush of angry feelings, a switch that broke before I started to beam with rage. I paused to consider the feelings of anger and the way they seemed to erupt. And after madness, there was more sadness.

I left the secure building that I worked at later that day and returned to my car, driving away to a distant parking lot with no one around. I called behavioral health at the hospital and tried to get a sentence together to say what was going on. Feelings overtook me, and I struggled to answer basic questions to identify myself. Patient and very concerned, a psychologist was brought to the call and just listened. I feared my conversation and disclosure would put my security clearance at risk. With assurances that it was a safe place, I still felt a sense of guilt for having to tap out. She listened and gave me permission to unfold what I felt and exchanged ideas about what could be done next.

Formally retired from the military, I began to work in a new role in cyber security in the private sector and begin this new chapter in life. So much to be grateful for. There was more time, the morning wakeup was not so extreme, and I had more latitude in civilian work to prioritize my responsibilities. On weekends, I was able to enjoy walks and time with my wife that we had missed during the previous years. I was on a journey with behavioral health and had transitioned to the VA for care. They pulled every lever to ensure there was continuity in care.

Augusta, Georgia, benefits from two VA facilities, and I drove to the smaller to meet with my assigned medical provider. From the parking lot, I marveled at the assortment of old men who were making their way to the front door. Some wore black ball caps with embroidery indicating their service and duty while serving. The information desk saw I was puzzled when I entered and quickly came to the hallway to greet me and point to the clinic I needed. The man in the red jacket pointed down the long hallway lined with service flags from the Army, Navy, Marines, Air Force, and Coast Guard. They were perfectly aligned with a window adding light to the display and dimensions of this long hallway.

The meeting with the provider was comprehensive, a chance to ensure they were caring for any of the mental health concerns. As the appointment ended, I aimed for the long hallway from the elevator. The flags were at a distance when I heard the piano play. Halfway down the hallway to the flags, a grand piano was indented into a space across from the service emblems. A bag sat next to the stool where a volunteer leaned into the keyboard and played the keys. The sound carried and bounced from the walls, greeting me as I approached. She played with abandon, neither the slightly out-of-tune notes or the occasional missed key subtracted from her intent. Walking closer, I saw the piano player swaying from side to side and continuing to play with great passion. Chairs lined the windows down from the well-appointed service flags. Savoring the piano music and its recognizable melody, I paused and sat to fully take in the sounds. The keys moved quickly and the movement of the pianist seemed to lever in order to make the music emanate from the sound board. She played a version of the popular Cold Play song aptly called "Fix You."

I thought of the emotional chorus of the song, and this poignant moment to reflect:

> Lights will guide you home
> And ignite your bones
> And I will try to fix you

Sitting as the sole listener and audience to this melody, I stayed until it was complete and then walked further to approach the bench. "Thank you for that," I said, considering how it seemed perfect for the moment and that I was fortunate to actually hear the song. She looked to me, slightly surprised by my approach, as she exhaled and nodded. I wondered how it was that she had played it so deeply, so carefully, and with such passion. She made no reply and simply sighed, lowering her head to absorb my comments with a slight smile before I began walking again. Carrying my pharmacy bag and appointment reminders, I came to the end of the hall and exited the front door.

CHAPTER 17

Strategies

A VOLCANO IS NOT JUST a volcano when it erupts. It looks like a mountain. But it's much more. Deep inside the Earth's crust, at a great distance to its top, a volcano's inner layer is composed of magma, the fiery liquid substance that travels via subterranean layers. Lots of rock, clay, dirt, and foliage decorate its outer crust. The eruption is only a season, a culmination of activity sparked by movements baked into the planet and not seen from the surface. At a distance, everyone would agree they see a mountain completely formed and with its own permanence.

Inside each of us there are the elements of a volcano; the parts we think we see and understand and the much larger hidden energy and form that spews out in crisis.

Understanding the composition and mechanics of a volcano may not bring us peace, but it is a useful way to examine how our fears, anxiety, and emotions bubble up in our life. As survivors, we put a lid on the eruption, calming at the surface, and many times reject the angst that persists deep inside. Just like the volcano, the heat of crisis fuels movement and changes that rise to the top. We want to believe we have put these negatives under a cover, and yet many times our life brings them out in other ways. We cannot overpower and suppress the volcano. The magma of our own emotions moves without restraint or pause.

Keeping secrets in my life created an enduring magma, a sticky milieu of issues I was unable to resolve alone. My words were jumbled before the age of ten, a stutter created inside the mechanics of my own development. Before high school, I had ulcers that were painful and yet did not steer me away from alcohol. I created an outer shell that looked like one thing but knew that inside it was much different. I gladly wore a uniform, savoring its meaning and hopeful for its potential to cure. The helmet protected me from harm but served as an incomplete shield to the lasting impacts of PTSD inflamed by service. Each of the turns and twists we naturally face added gravity to the underlying hurt from my youth. Challenges and adversity we experience further shape and define our reaction to the volcano created by childhood and life trauma.

Learning to cope and move forward from a crisis involves a multi-layered approach. We can see the solutions we seek first, but we can also find ways to mitigate the corrosive angst that persists. Over time, I developed more unhealthy approaches to my own circumstance. More recently, and with the benefit of therapy and some time of reflection, I offer a few strategies that others may find useful.

SURVIVE

A dear friend wrote to me from prison to explain his first days leaving civil society and entering the dungeon of jail, daily threats, and persistent danger. He provided critical advice that applies to all of us in crisis. When we are first thrown overboard and into the deep water, the shock causes us to quickly move using our arms and legs. Our instinctive response preserves our life, and we struggle.

We can tire and be ineffective at swimming or keeping above the water. Our head dips under and we spit the water from our mouth. We gasp for air. We kick our legs and move our arms furiously to tread water. We dip under again. And fight again.

In a crisis, our instinct is to fight to survive. We bob up and down in the water and struggle to keep afloat. We take deeper breaths when we can. We keep moving.

Soon we look around and notice that our head is above water. We have survived being dumped into the water. And we bob up and down, adjusting our water movement to keep our head up. If we persist, we can look to the horizon where we will soon see the beach. There is land next to the turbulent water.

The prisoner's perspective resonates. What we see and do in crisis merely gets us to the next moment. We learn to keep our head above water. The strength to move our limbs comes from somewhere else. We may struggle, but it is there. If we continue to work, kick, and focus, we will see the horizon and our sought-after beach. Until then, we must tread water.

SEE WHERE YOU ARE

Years after the childhood and military trauma were over, I was led to digesting these painful memories again, a pattern that drew me back to fear and hopelessness. In allowing myself to focus on the past, I too often missed the present.

As we can suffer from sweeps of anxiety, we are many times drawn back into the panic of previous trials. We relive a moment. We drag ourselves through the guilt one more time. We feel like it just happened. In these moments, we can make a deliberate choice. We can take a moment to study our surroundings and detail everything we think and feel. We can inventory what is actually happening and where we are. Then, in a deliberate way, we can determine whether we are actually reliving the trauma or if we are simply being brought back to the feelings.

We must consider the evidence. If we face harm, we instinctively move away. But absent that need to fear, we can move ourselves to examine our physical presence and think more deeply about where we are. We can then distinguish the two places: the one we feared that is not actually with us, and the place where we are and remain safe. We can then be ever more grateful for that very moment, the time we again recognized that the incident is over and does not linger. Our feelings recycle, but we have gratitude for safety and all that brought us forward, each day at a greater distance, from the horrible thing of the past. We are then present where we are.

PLAY MOVIES

In reflection and therapy, my broken and painful moments were examined in some detail. Guided meditation, talk therapy, and journaling elaborated the experiences again in a safe and supportive container.

Asked what I was thinking when I was first touched, I remembered that, in the panic, I felt myself depart from the flesh with my eyes squinting and head ringing loudly. When the touching persisted and fear overtook me, I searched my mind for a corner of refuge and a way to think of anything, anything at all, where I could center my thoughts and hide. When the deafening boom and flash of war came back to my alarm, the pixels of black and white covered my thoughts. In the torment, I created a movie theater and library of thoughts I could draw from when I needed to depart.

Each of us has a favorite scene or a movie that evokes special meaning and something we appreciate. It may be the resolution of conflict, achieving a great goal, or the recognition of true love. In each of these scenes, we add dimensions as we consider the ways each part resonates: the actors' lines, the setting, and the way the director pieces all of it together. Because we naturally have favorite scenes, we can convert this for our own use and meditation.

Take a moment to consider one of the favorite scenes in your life. Pause. Inventory every detail. Consider any of the people and each facet of the scene, even how it smells. Now place yourself as the director and prepare to start the replay. If possible, think of how the scene might look in slow motion. And because you are the director as you replay it, you can elongate parts that you really enjoy. The volume, the tempo, and the lights are all within your command as you prepare to play your favorite scene(s).

As waves of sadness or fear approach us, sometimes it is helpful to have a place to go. In reflecting on our favorite scenes, we orient to gratitude for moments we have had in real life. Being grateful for the best scenes can then overtake our consideration of memories that can come back as a weapon to tear us down. Reflections and meditations do not need to be complex and can adapt to any available time frame and any location where we are present.

What are your favorite scenes? How can you remember one sequence or moment and imagine it again to carefully consider each detail? Why is this remembrance important, and why does it merit your appreciation?

SEE THE IRONY

One of the common attributes of people who have trauma in their life is that the event(s) create a recurring and punishing pattern of thoughts. Herein lies the irony. People that are hurt in this way desire most that their hurt not be revealed. As a result, they keep its pain and infection a secret. They do so at great cost to themselves personally, subduing their own fears of recurrence and with the passion to sacrifice in order that this trauma not be known to others. The shame, they believe, would outweigh the hurt of what they have experienced.

The irony is that inside the mind of the hurt person, they ruminate and churn over the details and consequences of what happened. Endlessly. Thoughts of what went wrong, how they were at fault, and fear of being hurt replay without pause. This unrelenting narrative that a person endures can bring them to new lows and be a catalyst for depression if not resolved. In this way, the secret actually persists and takes shape in something that is not forgotten, not hidden, and not safe from harm. Oddly, the dark narrative, with all its hurt, is often repeated to the victim in a dangerous loop that, over time, can manifest itself in other ways. The challenge of keeping the secret is in changing the voice and rumination internal to the victim.

ACTION

Many therapists (not all) recommend ways to come to terms with a person's dark secret. This takes the form of writing, meditation, or action plans to unveil the truth. For now, consider the viability of the secret itself and decide if there will be a day when the secret is no more. Identifying this truth, the fundamental trauma-fueling pain, can pause the negative retelling and become a turning point for our own self-perception. And the best part, the victim makes the choice of how and when this happens. Lacking that, an unlocked version, the secret sustains its eroding pattern belying the word indicating "a thought captured and not shared" to one thought that burns a hole in our soul.

I knew my strategies were incomplete in a number of ways. They are biased by my own experience. They are not professionally developed. They seem tied to Earth. These strategies could never meet the needs and hurt of a wider audience. I studied my issues with forensic detail and sought the expert advice only after I failed to resolve any of it on my own. Years of planning and operational experience gave me incomplete answers. The master's degree in strategy I earned from the United States Army War College did not outline my way forward. A certification as a professional in project management gave little road-map for the next steps.

The goal of the sculptor, the artist slowly whittling their piece, is to shape and reduce the material in a way that brings to life their art. At some level, this is the same endeavor as an individual who attempts to perfect their being by scraping away parts that no longer belong. The process can truly create something new from the raw material, giving way to a design and look not known before.

As individuals, it is always better to know our limits, and where our wishes meet with reality. Can we whittle away the less attractive and unwanted parts of our experience in order to become something we prefer? Do we possess the ability to change in that way? What are ways that we can carve and whittle without losing material essential to our being?

Self-correction is the aspiration of many, and yet it seems inherently limited by its author. That is to say, to the extent we believe we can remove every blemish, we become constrained to the solutions we find ourselves and the ability, limited as it may actually be, to see the parts that need carving. We find ourselves critical, perhaps endlessly, creating a cycle of low self-esteem that can soon lead to hopelessness.

Heading into sixth grade, our projects for art class grew ever more complex. Instead of simply painting or coloring, in one semester, we were taught about Terrariums. The concept of the sealed container terrarium was that plants kept inside would continue to grow. The jar, so the theory went, created a sustainable environment for the plants. In creating our individual piece, each student had a mason jar and then roamed the schoolyard looking for moss, small plants, and sticks. We placed each of these items carefully into the jar and then carefully sealed it with plastic. To each top there were a small number of holes added so that air could slowly move through the top.

Impressive as the terrarium looked once created – carefully-laid green moss placed next to a wooden stick with other vegetation – the duration the project would last was measured in days. What first appeared as a transparent and mystical view of nature soon failed. Although it was true that the warmth indoors created condensation that would keep the moss moist and growing, the algae and fungi grew in the same conditions. What began as a container capturing the elements of green things that grow soon morphed into a jar of spoiled plants and rotting moss.

Disappointing as it was to see the terrarium fail, it was evidence that we could not sustain conditions for growth while isolating the plants from their native environment. The system artificially created inside the glass jar did not account for the worms that fed the soil and created a viable base for the moss. The wind that dried ground after rain was not present inside the project jar. The enduring need of plants to have nutrients and airflow from nature outshines our artistic desire to recreate it and make it portable in a jar.

In adjusting to the world around us to include our trauma and best moments, we are better cared for by leveraging the support we see around us. Our problem is not best kept in a jar. The fixes that we can create for the moment are unable to resolve our challenges in the long term. We each need the natural sunlight and moisture given to us in our daily lives. Boxing it up is certain to make it spoil.

SURRENDER

If we believe in another author, our Creator, then we have an avenue to understand more completely who He created. We might even accept His authority that we were created especially and not imperfectly to allow for the life we are to live. And that it is lived with imperfections. And injustice. And hurt. And then, that He uses our flaws and pain we have for a purpose greater than what we comprehend.

Infected by years of trying to self-correct and modify who I was, I came to surrender to the hands of the Creator when there was nowhere else to turn. I could not accept the injustice of what happened to me and see that as part of an omniscient God. But my argument against or inability to grasp that truth was just my stubbornness. If He is omniscient, then everything that happens is ordained by Him and known to Him even before it takes shape.

His decisions are based on a justice He requires in order to accomplish His will on Earth and not mine. He used the infection of childhood trauma just like He uses fire to clear a forest or an earthquake to reshape land. Volcanoes cause fire and forever change the landscape where they reside. What looks like fracture and burning ash today will look differently into the future.

Unable to reconcile that my loving God would ever allow me to be hurt at such a young age, I have grabbed at anything I thought would work to fix it. And resentment grew that I was spoiled by an injustice. I resisted any suggestion that my fire and volcano may also fuel something else.

As time passed and my pursuit of understanding these scars did not render understanding, I paused to consider that I was indeed left without an ability to see it or solve it completely. I admitted that there was one place for that: at His feet.

Perhaps God used trauma, difficult as it is for me to accept, to create a yearning for His help in my life. Without that gap, I may have considered myself capable of filling in that hole, satisfying the pain and removing this ugly part of me. I never succeeded. In fact, me trying harder to remove the blemish carved new holes and created new problems and consequences. I learned to rely on Him as the great healer and comforter. I was not made to rely on myself and be satisfied that my humanity could be resolved by my work alone. There was so much more.

Given the strong religious teaching in my childhood, I resisted the truth that God can and does use all things for His good. My sense was to strive to be the better person and then to pray when I got it wrong. My job, or so I thought, was to remove and cover the weakness so that I could be made acceptable for an almighty God.

I learned that perspective was wrong.

I skimmed over a number of Bible verses hoping to find one that would resolve what I saw as incongruent: the omniscience of God, and yet, His allowing me to be violated. I knew that I was made weaker from this occurrence and certainly the cascading impacts in my own decisions and mistakes. But I missed the verse about what God does with weakness.

> But he said to me, "My grace is sufficient for you, for my power is made perfect in weakness. Therefore I will boast all the more gladly of my weaknesses, so that the power of Christ may rest upon me."

> 2 Corinthians 12:9

I learned that weakness is an avenue for God's work in my life. In fact, I could admit and even celebrate my weakness so that His work could be done. Doing so would bring me peace. I learned that trauma need not be a secret we attempt to protect and hide in a terrarium. He is sufficient. His power is found in our weakness. His power can "rest upon me" if I am willing to live a life with no more secrets. There was never a moment when God was not aware of the harm done to each of us at some point in our life. He used that, and planned it and allowed it, because doing so achieves His will. I rely on Him in my weakness.

In the mornings now when I step into the pool, moving my arms, as I lean forward to form the first stroke, causes the first wave from the morning's calm. The mirrored plane of the water's surface is decorated by the newly formed concentric circle and wave's movement. The water is warmer by more than twenty degrees from the cold tub, generating tingling in my hands and a pleasant thaw for my torso. I move slowly to swim to the deeper end, seeing the first wave from the calm push its shape in front of me, reminding me of the counselor's meditation. Her words guiding me through a scene of reflection ended with the sunset, calm water stirred by a small droplet. Each movement has an equal and opposite reaction.

The angst that I felt when this dip began is now moving from me, pushed by the exercise of breathing and water. The challenge of the cold immersion allowed me to learn to slowly exhale, resisting my fight-or-flight response.

Shaken from sleep years before, I confessed first to myself that I was haunted by one man's hands when I was young. Over time, my attempts to camouflage became more elaborate but remained ineffective. In reconciling the hurt, I committed to acknowledging the root and the foothold this sin had taken in my life. In a poem, and in the days since that dark night, I see the small boy through the lens of a grown man free from the harm that once took him and later fueled my own faults. I see God's hand in sustaining me, even more when I am weak and even when I fail to abide.

To Him, it was always true that there are no more secrets. Living my life in that truth, I find joy in surrendering with wonder to the transformation He creates.

CHAPTER 18

Reflection

MIKE, MY FAITHFUL ALLY AND German Shepherd, is slower now, with hips that hurt and ears succumbed to the spoils of infection, causing them to curl. He does not long for the walk that I relied on to spark my day, seeing him trot to the fences for the tennis ball. When feeling his best, he finds the toy from the floor and jaws it slightly, sometimes squeezing it enough to squeak. He has taught me to pause and gratefully consider my resilience.

My sincere wish is that these pages have found a way into the thoughts of all those whose childhood hurts persist. For those broken in circumstances that created an unending war, I pray you may one day see peace. May this be an invitation to safely unveil brokenness that brought us sorrow but can be translated to good. If we squint our eyes, we can see there are many colors, reflections, and beautiful pieces. At a distance, it seems like a complex mosaic that we don't completely understand, but we see light and, perhaps, great hope. We forgive ourselves and surrender to something akin to the cold, a startling response that we resist and yet a way to see how we are each gifted with an ability to get warm.

I pray for your weakness, that you may one day see the magnitude of God's ability to give you great power to endure and to be made whole. And while we remain curious on Earth, that one day we see the amazing way He used broken crayons to unveil a portrait of unmatched beauty.

I offer this prayerfully with hope that brightness will be seen, secrets will unfold, and that footsteps going forward are liberated for a purpose greater than ourselves.

There is no song that describes all that has happened. Even so, let there be no more secrets.

CHAPTER 19

From the Window

Looking through fogging glass
Yearning for darkness to fade
Resigns me to my broken pieces
Weakness I covered with charade

I am but a log placed for splitting
Clear lines of frailty formed that way
His design linked to life's melody
A meaning I could not convey

Born a limb with many branches
Knots and turns formed by life
I consider now the majesty
Seeing weakness used to remedy strife

Split apart by a darkness
I found solitude in surrender
A prism casting light to my broken existence
Resigned, I learned to see the Father

A winding road to uncover

The truth placed plainly in Word
A life lived with a secret
Discovered the One who heard

ABOUT THE AUTHOR

The youngest of four children, Adam grew up in the lower-middle-class suburbs of Chicago and took on two paper routes hoping to one day earn his escape. Joining the military at seventeen at the lowest rank, he ascended through eleven promotions, rising to Brigadier General and Director of Operations for the United States Army Cyber Command. A published poet and magazine author, *No More Secrets* is his first book and a compelling way to unveil dark secrets kept while serving in uniform. Currently working as an executive in a cyber security consulting firm, he lives in Georgia near the Savannah River and enjoys long walks with his aging German Shepherd.

WAYS TO CONNECT

LinkedIn
https://www.linkedin.com/in/adamvolant/

Instagram
adamvolant.author

Website
adamvolantauthor.com

Bulk purchase of *No More Secrets* is available, with volume discounts for veterans and first responders. If interested in meeting with the author for speaking engagements, group facilitation, online discussion, or conference presentations, please utilize the contact information listed above.

www.ingramcontent.com/pod-product-compliance
Lightning Source LLC
Chambersburg PA
CBHW020234130626
46549CB00005B/1885